THE CURE FOR LOVE

A Lancashire Comedy
in Three Acts

by
WALTER GREENWOOD

SAMUEL   FRENCH

LONDON
NEW YORK TORONTO SYDNEY HOLLYWOOD

ISBN O 573 01084 5

MADE AND PRINTED IN GREAT BRITAIN BY
WHITSTABLE LITHO LTD., WHITSTABLE, KENT

THE CURE FOR LOVE

First produced (under the title "Rod of Iron") at the Oldham Repertory Theatre, on January 29th, 1945, with the following cast of characters:

(In the order of their appearance.)

MILLY SOUTHERN	*Molly Lawson*
MRS. JENKINS	*Alison Bayley*
JANEY JENKINS	*Joy Rowson*
SARAH HARDACRE	*Maude Lambert*
CHARLIE FOX	*Harry Lomax*
TED MUNTER	*Peter Willard*
JACK HARDACRE	*John McKelvey*
HARRY LANCASTER	*Maurice Hansard*
BARMAID	
MRS. DORBELL	*Hilda Knight*
JOE TRUMAN	*Norman Wynne*

The Play produced by DOUGLAS EMERY

After a preliminary provincial tour the play was presented by MR. ROBERT DONAT'S Company at the Westminster Theatre, London, S.W.1, on July 12th, 1945, with the following cast of characters:

MILLY SOUTHERN	*Renee Asherson*
MRS. JENKINS	*Dorothy Dewhurst*
JANEY JENKINS	*Joan White*
SARAH HARDACRE	*Marjorie Rhodes*
CHARLIE FOX	*Jack Rodney*
TED MUNTER	*William Heilbronn*
JACK HARDACRE	*Robert Donat*
HARRY LANCASTER	*Charles Victor*
BARMAID	
MRS. DORBELL	*Iris Vandeleur*
JOE TRUMAN	*Alec Faversham*

The Play produced by H. K. AYLIFF

SCENES

The action of the play takes place in Salford, towards the last stages of the second world war.

ACT I. Mrs. Hardacre's kitchen-living-room.

ACT II. SCENE 1. The Private Bar of the "Flying Shuttle".
SCENE 2. Mrs. Hardacre's kitchen-living-room.

ACT III. The Private Bar of the "Flying Shuttle".

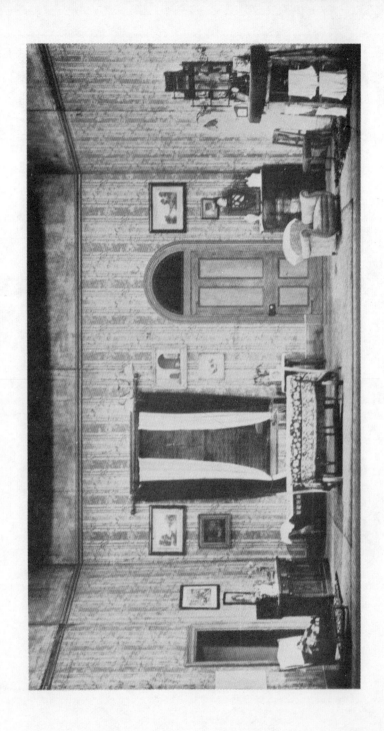

ACT I

SCENE: MRS. SARAH HARDACRE'S *kitchen-living-room. Towards the last stages of the second world war. It is afternoon.*

Up L. C. *is the door to the street. Down* R. *is a door to the scullery and other rooms of the house. There is a sash window with heavy curtains up* R. C., *with a sofa beneath it. Above the scullery door is a sideboard; in the corner up* L. *is a chest-of-drawers with a radio on it. There is a fireplace down* L. *with a kitchen range, and a clothes horse on which some of* MILLY'S *underclothes are airing stands in front of it. Above the fire is an upright chair over the back of which hangs* MILLY'S *skirt. Slightly* R. *of* C. *is a kitchen table with chairs above, to* R. *of and below it. There is an armchair down* R. *and a large chintz-covered easy chair before the fire.*

(See the Ground Plan and Photograph of Scene.)

When the CURTAIN *rises* MILLY, *in her underclothes, is above the table ironing her blouse. The radio is on.* MRS. JENKINS *and* JANEY *cross the window from off* R. *They knock on the door up* L. C. JANEY *returns to the window and knocks on it. There is more knocking on the door.*

MRS. JENKINS *(outside)*. Let us in. Let us in.

(MILLY *crosses to the fire, puts the iron on it, moves up to the chest-of-drawers and switches off the radio, then turns to the door.*)

MILLY *(unlocking the door)*. Whatever's the matter, Mrs. Jenkins?
MRS. JENKINS *(pushing the door open)*. Why've you got the door locked? Open it. Open it.
MILLY. What's up?
MRS. JENKINS. Out o' the way. Out o' the way. Let us in.

(*She pushes her way inside. She is followed by her daughter* JANEY, *a girl of* MILLY'S *age.*)

MILLY. Whatever's the matter, Mrs. Jenkins? Is the war over?
MRS. JENKINS *(impatiently)*. Phoo! Why've you got the door locked? (*She stands up* L. C.)
JANEY *(coming down to the table)*. Oh! Look at her utilities! (*She crosses to the easy chair and sits on the arm.*)
MILLY. Is that any business of yours? (*She comes down to the fire, picks up the iron and crosses to the table.*)

JANEY. She's ironing.

MRS. JENKINS. So she is.

MILLY. Yes, ironing. (*She tests the iron, finds it cold, and crosses to the fire.*)

MRS. JENKINS. You'd no reason to keep the door shut, had you?

MILLY. Yes, a very good reason. To keep people out. (*She crosses above the table to up* R.) I happen to like a little privacy occasionally.

JANEY. You do if you've got something to hide.

MRS. JENKINS. Well, I don't think much of London if you keep your neighbours standing on the doorstep. Do you, Janey?

JANEY. I think like you, Ma.

MRS. JENKINS. Let them as likes it live in London. But it wouldn't suit me. Would it you, Janey?

JANEY. I'd rather be here, Ma.

MILLY. Oh! if only this war were finished and I were free of Mr. Bevin and his factories! You wouldn't see my backside for dust. Manchester! Rain! Rain! Rain! A clean blouse on one minute and filthy the next!

MRS. JENKINS. Now you can't. . . .

MILLY. Can't I? I tell you, you're all daft up here. Proper daft. But listen to me! I'm talking your way now. "Proper daft"!

JANEY. Who are you calling daft, Milly Southern?

MRS. JENKINS (*moving above the table towards* MILLY). You'd better not let Sarah Hardacre hear you speaking like this in her house.

MILLY. She'll tell me if she doesn't like it. I say you're all daft up here. Slaving endlessly trying to keep clean. *And* no baths in the house either. (*She moves down* R. *of the table.*)

JANEY (*imitating* MILLY *phonetically*). Barths!

MRS. JENKINS. Well, anybody could eat their dinner off the floor in my house.

MILLY (*crossing to the fire*). They're welcome. Give me a table any time.

MRS. JENKINS. Well, I don't know how you and Sarah Hardacre've stuck it so long. At one another like cat and dog, morning, noon and night.

JANEY (*rising and moving in to* L. *of the table*). It's the nights we've come about, Ma.

MILLY. Have you ever thought we might like it?

MRS. JENKINS. I'd put nothing past Sarah Hardacre. Not that *I've* anything to say agen her.

MILLY (*picking up the iron*). You'd better not say anything against her while I'm about. (*She gestures with the iron at* MRS. JENKINS *and then puts it back on the fire.*)

MRS. JENKINS. Keep your hair on. Keep your hair on.

JANEY (*crossing below the table and pulling out the chair* R. *of it for* MRS. JENKINS *to sit on*). Go on, Ma, tell her what we've come about.

MRS. JENKINS (*sitting*). Don't hurry me, Janey. Don't hurry me.
I'm coming to it.

JANEY (*moving above the table*). Jack will be here first if you don't
hurry up.

MILLY. Jack?

MRS. JENKINS. Yes. We've come about him.

JANEY. We're engaged, me and him. Before he went. Here's my
ring.

MILLY (*picking up the iron*). What is this? A guessing game? (*She
moves to the table.*)

(JANEY *sits above the table.*)

MRS. JENKINS (*astonished*). Do you mean to say you didn't know
him and our Janey was engaged?

MILLY (*ironing*). I don't even know who you're talking about.

MRS. JENKINS. Jack Hardacre, o' course—him as won the three
medals in the Eighth Army. He's on his way home.

JANEY. As good as here already.

MILLY (*putting the iron down*). I'm very glad to hear it. (*She stands
with her hands on her hips.*) But what's that got to do with me?

MRS. JENKINS. He lives here. That's what it's got to do with you.
You knew she had a son, didn't you?

MILLY (*relaxing*). Considering that there's hardly a shelf or a
mantelpiece in the house without a cup or something he's won on
it, I'd be pretty dumb if I didn't. (*She folds the blouse she was
ironing.*)

JANEY. There, Ma. What did I tell you?

MRS. JENKINS. Well, he's on his way here this very minute.
Three years he's been away. He's a hero, that's what I've told
everybody. Haven't I, Janey?

JANEY. You have, Ma. And we're . . . all the neighbours're——

MRS. JENKINS. I'll tell 'er, Janey. I'll tell 'er. (*To* MILLY.) You
should see 'em!

MILLY. Who?

MRS. JENKINS. The neighbours. All of 'em. Every one of 'em
putting flags out in the street. And Mrs. Harrison's lendin' her big
streamer. . . .

JANEY. A big streamer what. . . .

MRS. JENKINS. . . . stretches right across the street, it does. Saved
it from the last war, she did. "Welcome Home", it says.

JANEY. He'll be glad to be home. Three years. . . .

MILLY. Yes, I know. Three years he's been away and you're
engaged. You told me. (*She puts her hands on her hips.*) And I still
don't see what it's got to do with me.

MRS. JENKINS. He's coming here, isn't he?

MILLY. You keep saying so.

MRS. JENKINS. Well, there's only two bedrooms in the house.
He's too old to sleep in his Ma's room.

JANEY. And wouldn't want to, I should hope.

MILLY. Are you suggesting he should sleep in mine?

JANEY. Milly Southern, what a thing to say!

MRS. JENKINS. What! And him engaged to our Janey! His Ma would have something to say to that.

MILLY (*picking up her blouse and the iron, and crossing to the fire*). So should I. (*She puts the iron on the fire and her blouse on the horse.*)

JANEY. I should hope so. And we've come to tell you——

(MILLY *takes her skirt from the chair above the fire and starts to put it on.*)

MRS. JENKINS. I'll tell her, Janey. I'll tell her. There's a spare bed in our Janey's room you can have.

JANEY. We wouldn't offer it to everybody.

MRS. JENKINS. It's only as it should be, seeing as how Jack and our Janey's engaged.

MILLY (*stopping dressing*). I see. I'm just an ornament round here. One that can't look after herself.

JANEY. I don't think.

MRS. JENKINS. Well, what about it?

MILLY (*continuing dressing*). I couldn't be more comfortable than where I am, thank you.

JANEY. There——

MRS. JENKINS. You see—three years he's been away from civilization, remember.

JANEY. And good influences.

MRS. JENKINS. And that's you, Janey.

MILLY. Three years is a long time.

JANEY. What does she mean, Ma?

MRS. JENKINS. Trying to be funny, if you ask me. Never you mind, Janey. You've got that there ring, love . . . and don't forget.

JANEY. There was too much happened for me to forget, or him either.

(SARAH HARDACRE *crosses the window from off* R.)

MRS. JENKINS. Jack's the best-natured lad in the world, even if his Ma does rule him with a rod of iron. There'll be a change when he comes back now he's been away from home. Mark my words, there'll be a change.

(SARAH HARDACRE *enters up* L. C. *She is a middle-aged woman, neatly dressed, inexhaustibly energetic and a demon for work and system. She carries a shopping bag. She comes down* L. C. *and glances at the fire.*)

SARAH. Well—huh!

MILLY. What have I done wrong now?

SARAH (*putting her bag on the easy chair*). Half hundredweight of coal on the fire the minute my back's turned. Wait till you've got a home of your own, young woman. That'll teach you to watch points. (*She turns up to the chest-of-drawers.*)

MILLY. There's appreciation! After I've scraped all the slack from the coal heap!

MRS. JENKINS. You've heard, Sarah?

SARAH (*putting her hat in the* L. *top drawer of the chest*). Heard what?

MRS. JENKINS. Didn't the neighbours tell you?

JANEY. All the neighbours. . . .

SARAH. I don't stand gossiping to neighbours.

MRS. JENKINS. Your Jack's on his way home.

JANEY. Home on leave.

SARAH. Eh?

MRS. JENKINS. Aye! On his way home now, he is. Our Janey's that pleased. Aren't you, Janey?

JANEY. Ooo yes, I am, Ma!

(SARAH *looks at* MILLY, *then comes down to* L. *of the table.*)

SARAH (*folding the ironing cloth*). An' might I ask how *you* and all the rest of the street came to know? (*She puts the ironing cloth in the sideboard, takes out the tablecloth and puts it on the table.*)

MRS. JENKINS. Met our Harry out delivering telegrams. It's his job to seal 'em up at t'post office. Should be here with it any minute. He'd to take one to the mill first. Wouldn't give me yours to bring. I hurried here as fast as I could . . .

(*A band is heard off.*)

. . . and told our Janey and the neighbours.

JANEY (*rising*). There's the band tuning up! (*She crosses towards the door down* R. *singing.*)

MRS. JENKINS (*rising and moving to the window*). Oh, and I forgot. Brass band's turning out to join in the welcome home. Bit of Harry Lancaster's doing, that. And. . . . (*She moves down to* R. *of the table.*)

SARAH. Hold your noise, woman, for goodness' sake.

MRS. JENKINS. Ho! That's the way it is, *is* it?

SARAH (*crossing to the armchair down* R.). That's the way it is. And I'll thank you to keep your nose out of my business in future.

MRS. JENKINS. *Your* business! Hear that, our Janey?

JANEY. I wouldn't've believed it, Ma.

MRS. JENKINS. Your Jack'll have something to say about that when he comes in.

SARAH (*taking off her coat*). If you've said all you've got to say, then be off. (*She takes her apron from just inside the door down* R. *and hangs her coat in its place.*)

MRS. JENKINS. I haven't said all I've got to say.

JANEY. And she hasn't said nothing.

MRS. JENKINS (*to* MILLY). About that spare bed, miss.

SARAH (*crossing to* R. *of the table; to* MILLY). What's all this?

MILLY. I'm invited to move; you know, Sarah—respectability.

MRS. JENKINS. It's only right and proper.

JANEY. Right and proper, that's what I said.

MRS. JENKINS. Look at her. Only just put her skirt on. Half naked when we came in. She won't want to get washed and dressed at the sink with a soldier about the house.

JANEY. And trained to use their eyes soldiers are.

SARAH. When she's my age she'll like be complainin' because soldiers don't look at her. Anyway, I'm capable of running my house respectable.

(*She crosses* MRS. JENKINS *and* JANEY *and exits into the scullery.*)

MRS. JENKINS. H'm, I see. Making it awkward for our Janey, aren't you? Always been against the lass, always. But she's got his ring, remember. She's got his ring.

(SARAH *enters with a basin.*)

SARAH (*going to the sideboard*). He must have been mad. But he got himself into it. Let him get himself out of it.

(*She puts the basin on the sideboard and exits down* R.)

JANEY. What!

MRS. JENKINS. *That* he won't do. I'll see to that. One of the best, our Janey is. One of the best. *And* never been seen out—(*looking at* MILLY)—with Yanks.

JANEY. Or Poles——

MRS. JENKINS. Or Canadians . . . like some that could be mentioned.

MILLY. Yanks and Canadians know what's what.

JANEY. Oh, Ma!

(SARAH *enters and goes to the sideboard.*)

MILLY. Anything you want ironing, Mrs. Hardacre?

SARAH. I don't think so. (*She gets out the sugar bowl.*)

MRS. JENKINS. Never mind, Janey. I'll see you're done right by.

SARAH. It'd look better of you both if you'd waste less time gassing to neighbours. That doorstep and those window-sills of yours haven't been touched in three days.

MILLY. Rub it in.

SARAH (*emptying sugar from the basin into the sugar bowl*). And that'll do from you, madam.

MRS. JENKINS. That's finished it. We'll not stay here to be insulted. (*She crosses up* L. *to the door.*)

(JANEY *starts to follow, moving above the table. There is a knock on the door up* L. C. MRS. JENKINS *opens it. Enter* CHARLIE FOX, *the diminutive tout of* TED MUNTER, *the local bookie.*)

CHARLIE. Hullo, Mrs. Jenkins. I've got a telegram for thee, Mrs. Hardacre. Me and Ted met your Harry with it, Mrs. Jenkins. Good news, isn't it, Mrs. Hardacre?

SARAH. Have you read it? (*She comes down* R.)

CHARLIE. Oh aye! The whole street has. Ted took the telegram from Harry Jenkins. Told me to bring it round. Thinks a lot o' your Jack, does Ted. Made many a bright shilling laying the odds on your Jack, has Ted. What a left he's got! Phooh! What a left!

(*He strikes a boxing pose, and makes one or two left-handed jabs, shadow boxing.*)

MRS. JENKINS (*snatching the telegram from* CHARLIE). I'll left you, my lad. . . . Out you go! (*She moves to* L. *of the table.*) There's your telegram, Sarah Hardacre—— (*Throwing it down.*) Don't clean my window-sills, eh?

(CHARLIE *exits.*)

JANEY. You could eat your dinner off them.

MRS. JENKINS. We'll hear what Jack's got to say about that when he comes home.

SARAH. Go on out of it, you nattering old faggot.

JANEY (*moving to* MRS. JENKINS). And don't forget I've got his ring.

SARAH (*crossing below the table*). And take her and her engagement ring with you! (*She pushes* MRS. JENKINS *and* JANEY *back out up* L. C.)

MRS. JENKINS (*outside the door*). I know your game, Sarah Hardacre. I know what you've got up your sleeve!

(JANEY *and* MRS. JENKINS *go off* L. SARAH *slams the door, moves to the window and closes it.* MILLY *starts to put on the blouse she has just ironed.* SARAH *turns and sees her.*)

SARAH. Has that blouse been aired?

MILLY. No.

SARAH. Well, take it off, or you'll catch your death.

MILLY. What's happened? Don't tell me you *have* got a heart after all? (*She arranges the blouse on the horse in front of the fire.*)

SARAH. No, I want no invalid on my hands. (*She comes down to the table.*) And if you young woman had the sense to wear woollens next your skin in these parts, there wouldn't be half the divorces. (*She picks up the telegram and opens it.*) You let the men see too much too soon. (*Looking at the telegram.*) More than nine words, you see. Wasting his money again!

(*She crosses to the sideboard, picks up the empty basin and exits down* R.)

MILLY. Well, you don't seem very excited about your son's homecoming.

(SARAH *enters with the hot-pot.*)

SARAH (*moving in to* R. *of the table*). There's enough getting excited, by the sound of things.

MILLY. You're the funniest mother I've ever met.

SARAH (*putting the hot-pot on the table*). Maybe it's the funny son I've got. (*She turns to the sideboard.*)

MILLY. You haven't seen him for three years—do you realize that?

SARAH (*putting the sugar bowl in the sideboard*). I realize he joined up agen my wishes. Fifty pounds I paid premium for him to learn his trade. Ten pounds a week in a reserved occupation, that's what he'd ha' been getting now, an' his own bed to sleep in every night. But he's the kind that won't be told. (*Half to herself.*) Our Janey. What a life in store. Couldn't ha' chosen worse if he'd been drunk.

(*She exits down* R.)

MILLY (*tidying herself in the mirror on the mantelshelf*). He could break if off.

(SARAH *enters with a bowl.*)

SARAH (*entering*). I can see him doing it. Soft in the head, that's what he is. (*She moves to the table.*) Doesn't like hurting people. Anybody tells him a hard luck story, and they can have all he's got . . . the great booby. Like a leech, she was. He couldn't have a bath there in front of the fire without her hanging about. Wherever he went, *she'd* be there, hanging on. But, of course, he wouldn't listen to me. (*She prepares the hot-pot.*)

MILLY (*putting on her blouse*). What're you making?

SARAH. Lancashire hot-pot. His favourite.

MILLY. Isn't that lucky? (*She moves to the chair above the fire and gets her shoes.*)

SARAH. It's lucky I made it yesterday, but I've got to warm it up. Are you going out?

MILLY (*putting on her shoes*). Might do. The "Flying Shuttle" want me to play in their dart match. (*She leaves her slippers by the fire.*)

SARAH. Pubs. Dart matches. . . .

MILLY (*moving up to the chest-of-drawers*). Aren't you proud of your son? (*She picks up a book.*)

SARAH. Proud? What for?

MILLY (*coming down to* R. *of the easy chair*). The medals they say he's won. (*She sits in the easy chair.*)

SARAH. Nothing fresh. He's always winning things. (*She inclines her head towards the mantelshelf.*) Look at 'em—swimming, boxing, running, and goodness knows what. Place cluttered up wi' things like that. Never anything useful. And the only time he gets any money he gives it to that Janey. Well, *are* you staying in?

MILLY. You seem very anxious to get rid of me.

SARAH. It's the clean blouse.

MILLY. What about it?

SARAH. If you aren't going out, change into something else. Mucking it up when it's just been washed. Soap's rationed, you know.

MILLY. There you go! The trouble with all you North Country people is. . . .

SARAH. That'll do, now. That'll do.

MILLY. . . . you make yourselves slaves to work. People in London. . . .

SARAH. London! Ha! Don't know they're born down there. Pull the oven damper out and make yourself useful.

(MILLY *rises and moves to the fire and pulls out the damper.*)

It'll be a good job when the war's over, and those who don't belong here can go back to where they came from. (*She turns to the sideboard.*) People in the wrong place all over the world. . . . That's the trouble with wars. (*She puts salt and pepper from inside the sideboard on to the top.*)

MILLY. It can't come soon enough for me.

SARAH. Five years to beat the blooming Germans. Lend 'em money while our lads're on the dole . . . then fight 'em. That's what comes of lettin' men run things.

MILLY. You married one.

SARAH. He was a human sponge—he wasn't a man. Could have floated a battleship in the booze he supped in his time. I'll never allow another drop to come into this house.

MILLY. Why did you marry him if you knew he was a drunkard?

SARAH (*crossing above the table with the hot-pot and coming down to the fire*). I'll tell you for why. Because a seventeen-year-old girl on the sands at Blackpool's daft enough to believe all she's told. Shift clothes-horse for me.

MILLY (*moving the clothes-horse upstage to the fire*). Maybe our Janey told Jack the tale. (*She moves up to the chest-of-drawers and puts the book on it.*)

SARAH (*putting the hot-pot in the oven*). He'll have to tell her a better one to get out of her clutches. Phoo! roast an ox, that oven would. Open that window, love, and let's have a breath of air.

MILLY (*crossing to the window*). Perhaps we can give Jack ideas. (*She opens the window.*)

SARAH. It's a good shove he wants, not ideas.

MILLY. Three years from home is a long time.

(*The band starts up.*)

Even you might be surprised.

SARAH. Nothing would surprise me . . . not at my time of life.

MILLY (*coming down above the table*). Go on. You talk as though you were past everything. What about getting a couple of bottles of beer in for him?

SARAH. No booze comes in this house. (*She crosses to L. of the table.*) Besides, he was T.T. when he left. (*She takes the tablecloth and cutlery from the table drawer and lays the table.*)

(MILLY *exits down* R. *She re-enters immediately with two small plates and two glasses. She puts them on the table.*)

MILLY (*moving up to the window*). Oh, listen!
SARAH. What is it? Siren?
MILLY. No—sounds like a band.

(*The band off is now playing, "Conquering Hero".*)

Here he is!
SARAH (*moving the chair below the table to* L. *of the table*). Making a show of himself in front of everybody.
MILLY. What do you expect him to do? Drive to the back door, hidden in a taxi, and creep in?
SARAH. Taxis. He'd better not let me catch him chucking his brass about on that sort of thing.

(*The band grows louder.* MILLY *pokes her head out of the window.*)

MILLY. All the neighbours are running down the street. Oh, you should see how they've decorated it!
SARAH (*crossing below the table to the sideboard*). Come inside, Milly.
MILLY. Here he is! Everybody's shaking hands with him. (*She turns* L. *of the window to* SARAH.) Ooo, isn't it exciting!

(*The band halts outside the house, playing fortissimo and almost, but not quite, drowning the cheers. People are congregated under the window, and one or two put their heads inside to shout something to* SARAH. *Whatever it is they have shouted is lost in the din of the band.*)

SARAH. For shame, Milly Southern. Such behaviour!

(*She exits down* R.)

MILLY. Oh, Sarah—for goodness' sake—come on. Let's go and welcome him.

(SARAH *enters with bread and knife.*)

SARAH (*moving to the table*). I'll do nothing of the sort. Making a show of myself, indeed! (*She sits* R. *of the table and cuts the bread.*)
MILLY. Oh, how can you sit there! Come on! (*She crosses to the door up* L. C. *and opens it.*)

(*Enter* TED MUNTER, *accompanied by* CHARLIE FOX, *leading the way ceremoniously for* JACK. *They stand each side of the door,* MUNTER L. *of it,* CHARLIE R. MILLY *breaks to* R. *of easy chair: There are cheers outside.*)

MUNTER (*heartily*). Come on, Jack! Come inside, lad! Here he is, Mrs. Hardacre.
CHARLIE. The conquering hero. In you come, Jack!

(*There are more cheers.* JACK *enters. In addition to his equipment he is carrying two cardboard boxes. The band stops.*)

MUNTER. Quiet, quiet, let the dog see the rabbit.

CHARLIE. Shut up! Let him kiss his mother.

JACK (*coming down* L. C.). Hello, Ma.

SARAH. Hello, lad—back again? (*She rises.*)

JACK. Aye, back again.

MRS. JENKINS (*at the window, outside*). And what a welcome, Jack, when your Ma never came to the front door, and you three years away.

SARAH. You're there again, you old besom! Shut window, Jack.

MRS. JENKINS. No holding her, Jack, since they made her manageress of that British Restaurant.

SARAH. You jealous old faggot, you!

MUNTER. England, Home and Beauty!

SARAH. You've never been so well fed in your life.

MRS. DORBELL (*outside, through the window*). Come to t' "Flying Shuttle" to-night, Jack.

JACK (*moving up to the window and shutting it*). See you all at "Flying Shuttle" to-night!

CHARLIE ⎱ (*together*). ⎧ Now Jack, lad, what about the boss fixing up a scrap for you?
MUNTER ⎰   ⎩ Think about it, Jack. The old purse of gold!

JACK (*crossing up* L. C. *below chest-of-drawers*). Go on, shift—shunt. (*He puts the large cardboard box on the chest-of-drawers.*) Must I get my gun to you? (*He puts his kit on the floor and on the chair above the fire.*)

(CHARLIE *and* MUNTER *go out.* JACK *shuts the door.*)

SARAH. Well, don't stand there like a moon-struck calf. Sit down and make yourself at home.

JACK. Aye. I suppose I may as well. Place hasn't changed much, Ma.

SARAH. If you'd ha' been here in the blitz when I'd no roof and all the windows out, you'd have said it was changed a bit. Sit you down.

MILLY (*indignantly*). Aren't you two going to kiss one another?

SARAH. Go on with you. None of that slop. (*She turns to the sideboard.*)

JACK (*coming down to* L. *of the table*). We aren't very demonsterative in our family, miss. (*He pronounces "demonstrative" phonetically as written.*)

(SARAH *brings two plates to* R. *of the table and stands staring at* JACK.)

MILLY. Well, I must say, this is a fine homecoming for a hero!

JACK. Nay, I'm no blooming hero.

MILLY. Well, at least you can sit down. Your mother's asked you twice. (*She pulls out the chair* L. *of the table for him.*)

JACK. Aye, thank you. Feet're ready to drop off. Stood in the train all the way North. (*He sits and takes off his anklets. He notices his mother's eyes on him. Embarrassed, he rubs his knees self-consciously.*)

SARAH. You've filled out a bit, lad.

JACK. Oh, grub's all right. Plenty of sand in it till we got to Italy, then it was all muck and snow.

MILLY (*crossing to the chair above the table*). I thought it was all sunshiny there.

JACK. So did I. Proper disappointing, all muck and snow.

SARAH. Did you get wounded?

JACK. Oh, just a scratch or two here and there.

SARAH. Will they give you a pension for it? (*She moves down* R. *of the table with the plates.*)

JACK. I never thought to bother about it, Ma.

SARAH (*crossing downstage to the fire*). You great daft loon! What's the use o' getting wounded if you don't get something for it?

JACK. I tell you, Ma, I never thought to bother about it.

SARAH. What a head. Bet you never did what I told you, did you, now?

JACK. What's that, Ma?

SARAH. "What's that, Ma"? I told you to keep near the Generals, didn't I? Then you'd never have got hurt.

JACK (*throwing his anklets into the corner up* L.). You don't understand, Ma. In the army, you've got to do as the Generals tell you.

SARAH. What do you want Generals for, anyway? (*She puts the plates on the stove.*)

JACK. Well, you've got to have Generals, Ma, or there'd be no fighting.

SARAH. Then them's the first that ought to be shot. Wicked, it is, wicked. Where were you wounded?

JACK. Oh, Alamein, Tobruk, and. . . .

SARAH. Nay, nay, you fool. What part of your body?

JACK. Oh, me ribs and me legs.

SARAH. Well then, off with your shirt and let's be havin' a look.

JACK. What?

SARAH. Take your shirt off, I tell you.

JACK. It's only a scratch.

SARAH. I'm the best judge of that. I tell you take your shirt off.

JACK. Nay, Ma, I can't. Not with a young lady in the kitchen.

SARAH. If you'd come here a few minutes since you'd have seen her half naked. (*She crosses to* JACK.) Come on, now.

JACK. There's nothing to see, Ma. It's only a scratch, I tell you.

SARAH. Will you get off that chair and take that coat off when you're told?

JACK (*rising slowly and taking his coat off; apologetically to* MILLY). It's very embarrassin' all this is for me, miss.

MILLY. Don't mind me. This is a change in striptease.

JACK. All the same, it's a thing I don't like, Ma. (*He folds his coat ver carefully, in correct army fashion, and puts it on the table.*)

SARAH (*pulling at his shirt*). Less of the gab, less of the gab.

He takes SARAH *a few paces towards the easy chair, away from* MILLY
on whom he turns his back.)

JACK. Give over. It's not there, it's here.

SARAH (*sympathetically*). Eeee! Does it hurt you, love?

JACK. No, not really, Ma. Only a twinge or two when the
weather's on the change.

SARAH. Might have been in a worse place, that's one consolation. (*She grabs his shirt again.*) Here, just look at that wound,
Milly! An' he says he never thought of claiming a pension.

JACK (*pulling away from* SARAH *and moving above the table, tucking in
his shirt.*) Hey! Give o'er. It's nothin', Ma. I keep telling you it's
nothin'.

(MILLY *moves down* R. *of the table.*)

SARAH. Why, there's chaps in this neighbourhood been in the
army and out of it in six months. They managed to get a pension,
and never went out of the country, let alone being wounded.

JACK. Yes, Ma, but it's no use——

SARAH. Don't interrupt. Called up, they were, what's more.
Not volunteered, like you were daft enough to do. (*She moves to the
fire.*)

JACK (*coming down* L. *of the table*). It's no use fussing about them,
Ma. I'm not worrying. By gum, it's good to be home.

MILLY. I suppose we'll be introduced some time or other.

SARAH. Comes from Tooting near London, she does. Milly's
her name, she was sent up here to work in a factory. Billeted on me
by that Bevin fellow. She's got your bed. You'll be sleeping on the
sofa there.

JACK (*crossing below the table to* MILLY *and clumsily proffering his
hand*). Pleased to meet you, miss.

(MILLY *moves in to meet* JACK *below the table and they shake hands.*)

MILLY. Milly's my name, Jack. And I'm sorry I've got your
bed.

JACK. Don't let that worry you, miss. The floor'll suit me. I
couldn't sleep in a bed any longer.

SARAH. Well, that's the army for you. They get hold of a lad
you've brought up respectable, and send him home trained like a
pig in a sty.

JACK (*turning to* SARAH). Makes a man out of you does the army,
Ma. (*He moves up* L. *of the table.*)

SARAH. That's the daft kind of thing you would say.

MILLY. What's daft about it?

SARAH. If you don't know, then you're as daft as he is. Get some
water on the table for me.

(MILLY *exits down* R.)

SARAH (*crossing towards* R., *below the table*). By gum, I'd like to have that there General Montgomery in this kitchen just for five minutes.

JACK. Nay, Ma, don't you say anything about him, now. He's all right.

SARAH. Of course he's all right, you soft loon.

(MILLY *enters with a jug of water. She puts it on the sideboard, and sits in the chair down* R.)

Waited on like the Lord Mayor's fool; car as big as a bus to ride in. I'll bet he never gave up a job like yours to volunteer . . . *and* I bet he never sleeps on the floor.

JACK. You'd lose your bet. He does sleep on the floor, *and* he has the same grub as the lads.

SARAH (*moving to the sideboard*). Then all the more fool him, if he's the boss. (*She picks up the water-jug.*)

MILLY. Are you sorry you joined up, Jack?

JACK. No, I had to do my bit.

SARAH (*moving above the table with the jug*). Father all over. Father all over.

JACK. Well, I got to be a sergeant, Ma. And there's the three medals. (*He moves above the easy chair.*)

SARAH. Something else for me to keep clean.

JACK. There's the honour of it.

SARAH. H'm. Honour and half a crown'll get you a good dinner when you're hungry. How long are you home for?

JACK. Eh?

SARAH. When are you going back?

JACK. It's a good job it was you that asked me that.

SARAH. Now what are you on about?

JACK. All the lads, fed up to the teeth they are, every time they get a spot of leave and come home. First thing they hear. "Hello, home again. When're you going back?" Coming from blokes in civvy street, too. Well, I said the first chap that said that to me when I got home would get a swipe across the chops.

SARAH. Let me catch you fighting, that's all. Another thing. How's it you never got a leave in three years? Other fellows did.

JACK. We—ll——— (*He turns away.*)

SARAH. Didn't you want to come home?

JACK. You see—er———

SARAH. You've no need to start thinking up a lie.

JACK. I'm not thinking up a lie. (*He moves down to the fire.*) I got leave all right, once. Champion it was. (*He smiles to himself.*) Cairo, in Egypt. Good to be home, though. Fourteen days I've got.

SARAH. I know that, and then what?

JACK. Then I'm posted to the local barracks to train new recruits for a spell. (*He moves to* L. C.)

SARAH. That'll be a change, teaching some o' them that's stopped at home.

(*She turns and exits down* R.)

JACK. Don't worry about that, I won't stick that long. Glider pilot, that's what I've applied for. (*He crosses to* R. *below the table.*)

MILLY. Which regiment are you in?

JACK. L.F.'s.

MILLY. L.F.'s? What's that?

JACK (*gazing at her for a second incredulously; then with almost indignant pride*). Lancashire Fusiliers. (*He moves up and sits in the chair* R. *of the table.*) You know, the men that fought at Minden. You should have been with us on Minden Day, Milly. . . .

(SARAH *enters.*)

SARAH (*entering and crossing above the table*). Started drinkin'?

JACK. What?

SARAH. Started drinkin'?

JACK. Well, Mother, as a matter of fact. . . .

SARAH. No lying, now.

JACK. I wasn't goin' to lie. Explainin', that's all. In the desert . . . all that sand. Proper parched we got, and you couldn't always depend on the water.

SARAH (*up* L. *of the table*). Tut, tut.

MILLY (*rising*). Where's the harm in drinking? (*She moves up* R.)

SARAH. Nobody's asking you, miss. (*She crosses to the fire.*)

MILLY (*crossing upstage of the table to* L. *of the chair above it*). Oh, I see. I'm to wait until I'm allowed to open my mouth now. You're always trying to talk me down.

SARAH. Some folks take a lot of discouraging. (*She takes the hot-pot from the oven.*)

MILLY. If you think you'll ever discourage me, you're very much mistaken, Mrs. Hardacre.

JACK. Do you go on like this all the time?

SARAH}
MILLY} (*together*). Like what?

JACK. Arguing with one another.

SARAH}
MILLY} (*turning; together*). Arguing? I never. . . .

SARAH. Go on, then, young lady. Go on.

MILLY. No, you go on. It's your house. We all know that.

SARAH (*crossing to* R. *below the table with the hot-pot and two plates*). My house! It's more like Ernie Bevin's, the way he keeps dumping people on me.

(JACK *rises and stands by the upstage* R. *corner of the table.* SARAH *moves to the chair* R. *of the table and puts down the hot-pot.*)

MILLY. Oh, if you want to get rid of me——
JACK. Nay, let's have a bit of peace, shall we? (*He sniffs the air.*)
By gum, something smells good!
MILLY. Your mother's made you a hot-pot.
JACK. Well! I don't know. (*He sits in the chair above the table.*)
SARAH. Draw up to the scratch, lad. You'd better have a bit too,
Milly, before he wolfs the lot. Man off a horse, that's what he used
to eat before he joined up. Give him some water, Milly. (*She puts a
helping of hot-pot on a plate.*)
MILLY (*pouring out water*). I wanted to get you a couple of bottles
of beer in. (*She sits in the chair L. of the table.*)
JACK. Well, it would have been very acceptable.
SARAH (*warningly*). You're looking for trouble, young woman.
JACK. Young lady was only trying to make me feel at home.
SARAH (*pushing the plate at him*). Here, let this stop your clatter.
(*She puts another helping on a plate.*)
JACK (*setting to*). Brought you a present home, Ma. That over
yonder in the cardboard box.
SARAH. Wasting your money again!
MILLY. Well! Of all the ungracious. . . .
SARAH (*passing a plate across to* MILLY). That'll do, Madam.
That'll do.
JACK. Go on, Ma. Open it.
SARAH. Oh, get on with your dinner!
JACK. Go on, Ma. Open it.
SARAH. Wait till I wash my hands, now.

(*She bustles out down* R.)

(JACK *passes the bread to* MILLY *and takes a piece himself.*)

JACK (*shyly*). I'd have brought you something if I'd known you
was here, miss.
MILLY. That's nice of you, Jack, and Milly's my name.
JACK. Milly, eh! Nice name.
MILLY. Oh, I hate it.
JACK. Nay, now. It's very nice. What's it short for?
MILLY. Millicent.
JACK. Millicent—lovely. What's your other name?
MILLY. Southern.
JACK. Millicent Southern. Ay, aye! It's lovely. Excuse me——
(*Business with a hot mouthful and a drink of water.*) Do you like being
up here?
MILLY. No, I can't say I do.
JACK. Oh, I'm sorry about that.
MILLY. I like most of the people, though.
JACK. Do you? (*He indicates* SARAH *off* R.) Terror, isn't she?
MILLY. I don't think so.
JACK. Neither do I, but she likes to think she is. She put me
through the mill when I was a lad. Right up to the time I joined up.

MILLY. Is that why you joined up?

JACK. Oh, no! I wanted to do my bit, you know. I can see it all now, making me go to night school and technical college. It was all for my own good. All the same, she's a rare old tartar. (*He resumes his eating and nods towards the door down* R.) She's coming back! Look out!

(*Enter* SARAH. *She crosses below the table and up* L. *to the chest-of-drawers. She takes the parcel and crosses upstage to the chair* R. *of the table. She rests the parcel on the chair and tries to undo the string.*)

JACK. Aye, that's it, Ma. The one in the box. (*He offers her a knife.*) Here you are.

SARAH. We don't cut string in war-time. Easy to see you've been in the army—wasting. (*She removes the wrapping and reaches out a gaily coloured shawl.*)

MILLY. Oooo! It's wonderful!

JACK (*to* MILLY). Do you like it, miss?

MILLY. Who wouldn't?

SARAH. How much did it cost you?

JACK. About five quid.

SARAH. *Five pounds.* Ha! Fool and his money.

MILLY. I'll give you six for it.

SARAH. You'll do nothing of the sort.

MILLY. How much, then?

SARAH (*placing it carefully in the box*). It isn't for sale.

JACK. Don't put it away, Ma. It's for thee to wear.

SARAH. Wear it? You're daft. It's too good to wear.

MILLY. You . . . you aren't going to wear it?

SARAH. You heard what I said. (*She crosses upstage to the chest-of-drawers, and puts the parcel in a drawer.*)

MILLY. Well——!

JACK. Don't take any notice, miss—that's Ma all over.

MILLY. But what is she going to do with it?

JACK. Same as she does with everything else I buy her—save it.

MILLY. But what for?

SARAH (*crossing above the table to the sideboard*). Well, one of these days, you never know . . . you never know. (*She brings the tray to* R. *of the table.*) Come on, let's be having you. I've got other things to do without standing about waiting. (*She puts the tray on the table.*)

MILLY. For goodness' sake sit down and relax. You've finished work, Mrs. Hardacre.

SARAH (*crossing to the chest-of-drawers*). I'll have you know that I've to go to the British Restaurant to-night.

JACK. What's that?

SARAH. I haven't shown my menus for to-morrow. (*She takes the menus off the top.*)

JACK. What's all this about British Restaurant, Ma? Have you opened a business?

SARAH (*crossing upstage to* R.). Listen to the fool. (*She comes down* R.)

JACK. Well, Ma, I've been away for three years, you know. I don't know what's been happening. And I'd put nothing past you.

MILLY. It's a Government thing, Jack. Anybody can go in and get a meal at cost price. They've got them all over the country. Good idea, isn't it?

(SARAH *sits in the chair down* R.)

JACK. Sounds all right.

MILLY. You can never get into your mother's place for the crowds.

SARAH (*checking menus*). That'll do, that'll do. I've got nothing to lend.

MILLY. Don't be so modest. (*To* JACK.) She could get married to anybody on the strength of her cooking.

JACK. Could she? (*To* SARAH.) Are you thinking . . . ?

SARAH. That'll be quite enough of that. Unless you'd like me to fetch you a back-hander.

JACK. I was only asking.

SARAH. And I'm only telling.

JACK. After all, Ma—you aren't too old.

SARAH. Listen to him! I'll have you know I can give some of the young ones a run for their money.

MILLY. If you don't leave it too late.

SARAH. Young woman, when you know as much about men as I do, you'll know there's only one thing they never get sick of—and that *is* something to eat. (*She rises.*) Not what you're thinking!

(*She moves to the door down* R. *and takes her coat from just inside.*)

MILLY (*simulating shocked reproach*). MRS. HARDACRE!

SARAH (*moving to the upstage* R. *corner of the table*). And you can drop the innocence, young woman. I've heard some of you girls when you come in for your dinners. Girls of your years, know more than is good for you. (*She crosses upstage to the fire.*)

MILLY (*groaning*). Here beginneth the first lesson.

SARAH. It's the way you've been brought up. (*She hangs up the oven cloth below the fireplace.*)

MILLY. Oh, I can't do with this sermonizing.

JACK. Very nice hot-pot, Ma.

(SARAH *moves up to the chest-of-drawers, gets out her hat and puts it on. She leaves her coat on the chest.*)

MILLY. What sort of a life do you think our generation's had? Born just after a war, living through a slump, and then, when we ought to be having a good time, pushed away from home into a factory, or the A.T.S. or the W.R.N.S.

JACK. Could I have a little more hot-pot, Ma? (*He holds out his plate.*)

(SARAH *crosses to the table, ignores* JACK, *picks up the hot-pot and takes it to the fire.*)

MILLY. Never knowing whether the man you might have married will come home. Yes, then I suppose after the war everybody will expect all the girls to go home and "be nice" and carry on like Sunday School teachers, as though nothing had happened.

SARAH (*bending over the fire*). Oh, yes?

JACK. Could I have a little more hot-pot, Ma?

SARAH (*crossing to* JACK'S L.). Guts. You've brought your appetite back, I see. (*She takes his plate and returns to the fire.*) Oh yes, you've all been badly done to. Music while you work, picture shows, uniforms found, and more money than's good for you, some of you youngsters.

MILLY (*sarcastically*). The old story—and——

(SARAH *crosses back to* L. *of* JACK *with his plate full.*)

—needless to say, it was a thousand times worse when you were a girl.

SARAH. Commando training wasn't in it. Sheep's heads and good hidings, that's what they brought me up on. (*To* JACK.) There you are, love. Get it while it's hot. I've got to go out now. (*She goes up* L. *to the chest-of-drawers and puts on her coat.*) Will you wash up for me, Milly? And when you do, be careful, because that's my best china. (*She opens the door up* L. C. *and turns.*) Here, listen, you two. No shinanigin'.

(*Exit* SARAH.)

MILLY. Shinanigin'? What's that?

JACK (*uncomfortably*). Shinanigin'? Well—er—it's——

MILLY. Go on.

JACK. Well—er—just shinanigin'.

MILLY. We could keep this up for ever. Did she mean carrying on?

JACK. Aye . . . you know. Messing about. (*Apologetically.*) O' course, there was nowt like that on my mind.

MILLY. Wasn't there?

JACK. Ay. No. I'm not that kind of a chap.

MILLY. You've no need to boast about it.

JACK. Eh?

MILLY. You talk as though a girl ought to be pleased to hear it.

JACK. What?

MILLY. That you're not that kind of a chap.

JACK. Oh, it's the way you're made, I suppose. Milly——

MILLY. Yes?

JACK. As a matter of fact, you know. . . .

MILLY. What?

JACK. I knew you weren't that kind of a lass, the first time I clapped my e'en on thee.

MILLY. Oh, say that again!

JACK. What? I hope I haven't said anything that. . . .

MILLY (*laughing*). Oh, no, no.

JACK. Are you laughing at me? I can't help the way I talk, you know. I know I'm no gentleman like them that come from Tooting.

MILLY. Oh, Jack, please, you don't know what I mean. What you said, the way you said it. It sounded lovely.

JACK. Go on. . . .

MILLY. It did. Say it again, will you?

JACK. Nay, lass, I've forgotten what I've said.

MILLY. When you said about my not being that sort of a girl.

JACK. Do you mean, the first time I clapped my e'en on thee?

MILLY. Yes, say it again, will you?

JACK. Well, I knew you weren't that kind of lass, first time I clapped my e'en on thee.

MILLY. Yes, that sounds lovely. It sounds just like poetry.

JACK. Do you like poetry too? I'm very fond of it—my Dad taught me lots. Do you know:

> "Come, Mary, link thy arm i' mine,
> And lilt away wi' me,
> An' dry that little drop o' brine
> From the corner of thy e'e."

(*He puts a finger up to his eye.*) Eye. Same idea, you know. I could go on for hours. You know, Milly, you remind me of that poem.

MILLY. Do I?

JACK. Yes, you do.

MILLY. Jack, what made you think I wasn't that kind of a girl?

JACK. Well, I was hoping you wasn't, that's all.

MILLY. Why?

JACK. Nothing. I was just thinking.

MILLY. Well, do you think I am? Do you?

JACK. How long have you been living here with Ma?

MILLY. Over a year.

JACK. Well, Millicent Southern, there's nowt more to be said.

MILLY. Oh, I see. (*She rises, moves below the table with her plate, and puts it on the tray.*) If I'm all right by your mother, I'm all right by you. (*She puts the other used crockery on the tray.*)

JACK. Now what are you on about?

MILLY. Just that you sound as though you're the kind who can't make up his own mind.

JACK. Oh, I can't, can't I?

MILLY (*taking a glass to the sideboard*). I said it sounded like it. (*She returns to the table.*)

JACK. I made up my own mind about joining the army, didn't I? But don't let's argue, eh, Milly?

MILLY (*still clearing the table*). All right.

JACK (*rising and moving* L. *of the table*). Have a fag?

MILLY. Not just now, thank you.

(JACK *takes a cigarette himself, but does not light it. He eyes her up and down furtively.*)

JACK. Er. . . .

MILLY. Go on.

JACK. Are you married?

MILLY. No.

JACK. Courtin'?

MILLY. No.

JACK. Do you fancy anybody?

MILLY. No, I don't. And to save time, I'm twenty-two, I've got over a hundred pounds in war savings, and that chair. (*She indicates the easy chair.*)

(JACK *glances at the chair.*)

JACK. I hope you didn't think I was just being curious.

MILLY. Well, you know now.

JACK (*looking at the easy chair*). Is that your chair? Is it really? Might have guessed as much. Ma wouldn't go in for anything like that. Bet it's comfortable.

MILLY. Well, it's there. Try it.

JACK (*moving to the chair and sitting in it*). By gum. Can I sit in it? Can I? By gum, this is a bit of all right, this is. This is lovely. It's springy.

(MILLY *takes the tray to the chair down* R. *and rests it on it.*)

MILLY. Jack——

JACK. Yes?

MILLY. I've been thinking.

JACK. What about?

MILLY. I'll sleep on the sofa and you can sleep on the bed while you're on leave.

JACK. Don't be daft, lass. I've told you floor'll do for me.

MILLY (*crossing below table to the fire*). It wouldn't do for me. You like it comfortable, don't you? (*She turns to him, and stands with her back to the fire.*)

JACK. There's nothing to complain of. We didn't have any beds out there.

MILLY. Where did you do your fighting?

JACK. Oh, Alamein, Libya, Tunis and Italy.

MILLY. You fought all that way, and when you get home and there's not even a bed to sleep on you say there's nothing to complain of? Your mother's right, you *are* daft.

JACK. I dunno—those things don't matter. The fact of being

home again is quite enough for me. Be glad when the blooming war's over though and I can get settled down again.

MILLY. You'd better get some practising in the settling down while you're on leave. (*She crosses to the chair down* R. *and picks up the tray.*) You take the bed and I'll take the sofa.

JACK. I've told you, lass. . . .

MILLY. You heard.

JACK. Now look here, Milly. . . .

MILLY. No argument, either.

(*She exits down* R.)

JACK. All right—if you say so. I can see it's no use arguing. (*Almost aside.*) Bet I'll sleep on t'floor just the same.

(MILLY *enters with clean cutlery and lays a place above the table.*)

(*He sighs.*) Milly, do you know Janey Jenkins?

MILLY. I've seen her around. (*She turns to the sideboard.*) She was in here just before you came in. Why? (*She brings a plate to the table.*)

JACK. Nothing. I was just thinking. Just my luck, I suppose.

MILLY (*moving to the sideboard*). It'd be a good idea if you'd stop talking in riddles. (*She takes a needle and cotton from the workbasket.*)

JACK. Well, I couldn't help hoping, that's all.

MILLY (*taking her coat from the sofa and crossing to the chair* L. *of the table*). Hoping what? (*She sits and sews at her coat.*)

JACK. Well, you see, when I was in the desert, and Italy, some of the lads got letters from their girl friends, saying as how three years away is a long time, and they'd changed and found someone else, and—you know, Milly—good-bye and the soldier's farewell. You know what I mean.

MILLY. The post goes both ways.

JACK. Eh?

MILLY. If you felt that way about it, why didn't you write and tell her you'd changed your mind?

JACK. Aw, I'd got nobody else in mind . . . and a feller can't go and do a thing like that, can he?

MILLY. Do you mean to say that if you were engaged to me and then you found out that you weren't in love with me, you'd marry me just because you thought it was the right thing to do?

JACK. Well, it is, isn't it?

MILLY. You're mad. Absolutely mad. Spoiling two people's lives—is that the right thing to do?

JACK (*rubbing his chin thoughtfully*). I never thought of it that way.

MILLY (*impatiently*). Oh! Were you *ever* in love with her?

JACK. No—er—now I come to think of it, I wasn't.

MILLY. Then why did you buy her a ring?

JACK. I didn't.

MILLY. What? How the dickens did she get it, then?

JACK. Well, you see, she was always around, like. And it was her birthday, she said, and I'd won five quid at boxing, so I gave it to her and said, buy yourself something. A present, like. So she bought herself a ring.

MILLY. Do you mean to say she bought herself an engagement ring?

JACK. That's what she said it was.

MILLY. Well! And you said nothing, of course.

JACK. Aw—you know how it is. You don't like to hurt people. Besides, it's as I said. I didn't see anybody else coming along.

MILLY. Didn't it ever occur to you that somebody *might* be coming along?

JACK. No, it didn't. To tell you the truth, Milly, I ne'er thought I were much to look at.

MILLY (*rising and crossing to the sideboard with her coat*). Oh, what a fool you are! (*She looks for the scissors.*)

JACK. All right. All right. I know, Milly. But if you were a man, I'd knock your clock round for saying it. (*He rises and turns upstage.*)

MILLY (*using the scissors*). It's women you ought to watch, not men. (*She puts the scissors, needle and thimble back in the workbasket.*)

JACK. Fine time to tell me that, now I've put my foot in it.

MILLY (*moving below the sofa*). If you're going to stand for that, all I've got to say is it's lucky that they weren't women soldiers you were up against . . . or you'd have been in the soup. Anyway, it's no business of mine.

JACK (*above and* R. *of the easy chair*). I wouldn't be so certain of that, if I were you.

MILLY. Oh? Meaning what?

JACK. Meaning I've never met a lass like thee before. Never.

(*There is a knock at the door up* L. C. JACK *moves down to the fire.* MILLY *drops her coat on the sofa, crosses to the door and opens it.* HARRY LANCASTER *enters. He is well dressed, fifty-ish, paunchy and hard-headed. He carries his hat in his hand.*)

LANCASTER. Is she in?

MILLY. No. She said she wouldn't be long. Won't you come in?

LANCASTER. Aye, I don't mind if I do.

(MILLY *shuts the door.*)

JACK. Hullo, Harry. (*He stands with his back to the fire.*)

LANCASTER (*coming down* L. C.). Hullo, Jack, so you're back, then.

JACK. Aye, looks like it somehow.

LANCASTER. Aye. (*He stands at the upstage* L. *corner of the table.*)

MILLY (*crossing upstage to* R. *of the table*). Well, you've no need to act like the man from the Prudential. Sit down. There's no charge.

(LANCASTER *looks at the easy chair, hesitates and sits on the chair* L. *of the table.*)

LANCASTER. Aye, thank ye, miss. I don't mind if I do. (*He puts his hat under the chair.*)

JACK. Took quite a time to make up your mind about that.

LANCASTER. Yonder chair looks comfortable.

MILLY (*sitting in the chair* R. *of the table*). Then why didn't you sit in it?

LANCASTER. Matter of fancy. Tell you the truth, I'm rather surprised at her going in for anything like that.

MILLY. She didn't.

JACK (*indicating* MILLY). It's hers.

LANCASTER. Might 'a' guessed it. (*He looks slowly and appraisingly round the room.*) Clean as a new pin.

MILLY. What?

LANCASTER. Her house. Never seen a woman like her for energy. Rare 'un, she is. A proper rare 'un. How do you get on with her, miss?

MILLY. Very well indeed, thank you.

LANCASTER. Bit sharp on the tongue, isn't she?

MILLY. All barking. She doesn't bite.

LANCASTER. That a fact? Aye. Aye. O' course. Yes. Aye. H'm.

(JACK *lifts the lid off the hot-pot.*)

Good smell, isn't it? (*He rises and moves towards the fire.*)

JACK. Aye.

LANCASTER. Hot-pot, isn't it?

JACK. Aye. Hot-pot.

LANCASTER. Thought it was. She's a rare cook, isn't she?

MILLY. I think so.

LANCASTER. So do I. (*He moves to the fire and stands beside* JACK.) There's a fortune in her.

JACK. Who for?

LANCASTER. What d'you mean?

MILLY. You haven't got your eye on the fortune, by any chance?

LANCASTER (*with relish*). The old "Flying Shuttle's" my fortune, lass. Ahhh! The brass I've turned over since war began! I'm all right, don't fret yourself about that. It's too late for any feller to start thinking of making a pile if he hasn't done it by my time o' life.

JACK. With all the brass you've got, I should think it about time you thought of getting married. What about Mrs. Jenkins?

LANCASTER. Me? 'Er? Not bloody likely.

JACK. Here, Harry Lancaster, steady on, steady on. Ladies present.

LANCASTER. Beg pardon, miss.

MILLY. Oh, that's all right, I've heard it on the movies. Bernard Shaw, you know.

LANCASTER. Bernard Shaw? One of them there fancy fellows from Hollywood, I suppose. You don't catch me wasting my time on the movies. Aren't you going to the "Flying Shuttle", Miss?

MILLY. When I've done the washing up. (*She rises and moves to the sideboard.*)

JACK (*crossing up* C.). What are you going to the "Flying Shuttle" for, Milly?

MILLY. I'm in the darts team. We have a match on to-night.

JACK. Can anybody come?

MILLY. It's a free country.

JACK (*above the table*). That's true enough. I'll be there before you've got your first double.

(*He crosses above the table and exits down* R.)

LANCASTER (*moving towards* C.). Do you like him, miss?

MILLY (*coming down* R. *with some sewing*). Tell you better when I know him. (*She moves below the table to the* L. *end of it.*)

LANCASTER. Good lad, he is. Don't like her he's engaged to. She's a long time, isn't she? Where's she gone?

MILLY. British Restaurant. Arranging to-morrow's menus.

LANCASTER. Surprising, that. Her working there. She needs someone to set her up in business with a pie shop. That British Restaurant'd be bankrupt in a week. She's the Restaurant, tha knows. (*He moves in to* MILLY'S L.)

MILLY. Tha seems to know.

LANCASTER. Eh?

MILLY. I said, "Tha seems to know."

LANCASTER. Aye. Ah thought that's what tha said.

MILLY. Well, now tha knows, Ah did.

LANCASTER. Aye.

MILLY. Aye.

LANCASTER. Ee, sounded funny coming from thee. Never heard any of the lasses from the South speaking English before.

MILLY (*sitting on the table downstage* L. *corner*). If I stay here much longer, I shan't be understood when I get home.

LANCASTER. Come from London, don't you?

MILLY. Yes.

LANCASTER. I thought so. Went there once. Cup Final. Didn't think much of it. Not a patch on Blackpool.

MILLY (*getting off the table*). You don't mean to tell me that you've been in London?

LANCASTER. Oh yes, I know it well. Stopped there the whole day. Got in about seven in the morning. Had a look round 'til it was time for t'match. Then we had a bite in one of them cafes (*rhyme with "safes"*). Didn't half charge us, too. Glad to get on a train again at midnight. Beer was rotten and I didn't think much o' Buckin'am Palace, neither.

(MILLY *crosses to the sideboard and puts away her sewing.*)

(*He looks at his watch.*) She *is* taking her time, isn't she?

(*Enter* JACK. *He puts his foot up on the armchair down* R. *and ties up his shoe string.*)

JACK. Still here, Harry?

(MILLY *picks up her coat from the sofa and exits down* R.)

LANCASTER (*moving up* C.). Army life seems to agree with thee, lad, from look of you.

JACK. Might be worse. I'll be glad when I'm finished with it for good and can settle down.

LANCASTER. Do you mean get wed?

JACK. I dunno. (*He scratches his neck.*) I dunno.

LANCASTER. Chap's got to make a move in that direction sooner or later.

JACK. Taking thee a hell of a time. (*He moves in to* R. *of the table.*)

LANCASTER (*moving to the chair above the table*). Takes two to make a bargain, lad. (*He sits.*)

JACK. Sounds as though you've got your eye on somebody.

LANCASTER. Well. To tell the truth, there *is* a certain party. H'm. Aye. H'm. Fine lass yon girl who's staying here.

JACK (*glancing jealously at* LANCASTER). Get away, man, you're old enough to be her grandfather.

LANCASTER. Nay, Jack. 'Tisn't her I'm thinkin' of. No, there is a certain party I've been turning over . . . in my mind, you know. You're all right, though. Fixed up nice and proper.

JACK (*crossing above the table to up* L.; *gloomily*). I'm fixed all right.

LANCASTER. Your Ma'll miss thee when you go.

(JACK *grunts.*)

I'm surprised that young woman who lives here hasn't gone before now.

JACK (*moving in to* L. *of the table*). Gone where?

LANCASTER. Married. There was an American officer used to come in the "Flyin' Shuttle" a lot.

JACK. Was there?

LANCASTER. Always askin' after her, he was.

JACK. He was. Was he?

LANCASTER. Aye. Got posted away, he did. Don't think he made much headway. Good customer, though. Double whiskies and drinks all round. Same as that Canadian sergeant that was sweet on her.

JACK (*taking out his cigarette lighter, about to use it*). Oh yes! They get the brass, don't they.

LANCASTER. Foremen of the factory where she works is a regular customer there these days.

JACK. How old is *he?*

LANCASTER. About twenty-five. Good-looking feller. Anyway, you've no need to worry. You're fixed up.

JACK (*putting the lighter away and jabbing the cigarette behind his ear*). Turn it in, turn it in—(*he throws the cigarette into the fireplace*)—will you? Telling me all the time I'm fixed up. (*He crosses below the table to down* R.)

LANCASTER. Well, you are, aren't you?

JACK. If I am, I am, and I don't need to be blooming well reminded of it all the blooming time.

LANCASTER (*rising and moving to* L. *of the table*). I don't know what's up with everybody to-night. Snapping back every time you try to be pleasant. He's just as bad.

JACK. Who's "he"? (*He moves up* R.)

LANCASTER. Yonder foreman fella who's sweet on yonder lass in there. He's in the pub now waiting for the dart match to start. Watch the way he acts when he sees her.

JACK (*crossing above the table to* C.). If he tries any fancy tricks on while she's with me I'll give him a bat across the ear.

LANCASTER (*meeting him up* C.). Not in my pub you won't.

JACK. And anybody else who tries to stop me. Including thee, as old as you are.

LANCASTER. Old as I am? Old as I am? What d'you mean?

JACK (*crossing to the chair above the fire*). You'll find out, Harry. One of these days I'll be putting my foot down. (*He picks up his cap.*)

LANCASTER. You take my tip, lad, and let trouble come looking for you. Can't understand thy ma. Wonder what's keeping her? (*He moves to the window.*)

JACK. I wouldn't be knowing. I've been away three years, you know. I dunno what tricks she might have been up to. (*He moves* L. C.)

LANCASTER. She wrote to you regular, didn't she?

JACK. Aye.

LANCASTER. Then she must have told you all she was up to.

JACK. I wrote to her regular, but I didn't tell her all I was up to.

LANCASTER. Some women are dark horses, Jack.

JACK. Some fellers'd like to think *they* are, too.

(*Enter* SARAH *up* L. C. *She puts her hat on the chest-of-drawers, and her coat over the easy chair.*)

SARAH. What're you doing here, Harry Lancaster?

LANCASTER (*taking a step to* C.). Waiting to see thee, and I thought you ne'er were coming.

(JACK *clears over* R.)

The team's waiting for the young lady at the pub, Jack.

SARAH. Pubs! Dart matches——!

(*Enter* MILLY *down* R.)

MILLY. I'm ready, Jack. (*She crosses below the table and up to door, up* L. C.)

(JACK *follows.*)

See you later, Mrs. Hardacre.

SARAH. And think on. . . .

JACK. We know . . . no shinanigin'. Good night!

(JACK *and* MILLY *go out.*)

SARAH (*moving to the fire*). Well, Harry Lancaster—and what's on *your* mind?

LANCASTER (*crossing down* L.). Well, Sarah, you see. . . . Hot-pot smells good, Sarah.

SARAH. It ought to do—I've just warmed it up.

LANCASTER. You're a gradely cook, lass.

SARAH. That's not the first time you've told me that either.

LANCASTER (*ingratiatingly*). There wouldn't be a little bit left in the dish, would there?

SARAH. You can have a bobsworth.

LANCASTER. Nay—d'you mean to say you'd charge me for it?

SARAH. Do you give your beer away?

LANCASTER. Nay, Sarah, now—that's different.

SARAH. I've told you, you can have a shillingsworth. (*She takes the hot-pot off the fire and crosses downstage to* R. *of the table.*)

(LANCASTER *crosses to the chair above the table, sits and puts a shilling on the table.* SARAH *moves in to* R. *of the table, puts the hot-pot down and takes the shilling.*)

SARAH. And you needn't be undoing your waistcoat. You won't get that much. (*She puts a helping on his plate.*)

LANCASTER. Aha! (*He looks at his plate.*)

SARAH. Yes, it's my best china.

LANCASTER. (*He takes some bread.*) My, this is tasty, lass.

SARAH. Aye. I think I'll fetch a plate and try a bit myself.

(SARAH *exits down* R. LANCASTER *helps himself to more.* SARAH *returns with a common plate.*)

LANCASTER. Eh! Why didn't you use one of your best plates?

SARAH (*at* R. *of table*). One on table's risky enough. Just look at this thing. Utility. Daylight robbery, more like. (*She helps herself to hot-pot.*) Well now, what's on your mind?

LANCASTER. Well, Sarah—— (*He interrupts himself.*) You haven't got a drop of anything to drink in the house? A pint would go down well with this, you know.

SARAH (*sitting in the chair* R. *of the table*). You know better than to ask.

LANCASTER. I just thought like—Jack being home.

SARAH. Think again. Come on. What is it you've come round about?

LANCASTER. It's about Jack.

SARAH. What's he been up to?

LANCASTER. Nothin'. It's all the fellers at the "Flyin' Shuttle". Thought it would be a good thing if we gave him a do.

SARAH. Where?

LANCASTER. In the street. You know. My piano in the middle of the road, and few tables and chairs . . . everybody bring their own. Bit of singing and jigging. George Oakroyd says he'll play his English concertina.

SARAH. Fine goings on.

LANCASTER. Nay—the folk want to show what they think of your Jack.

SARAH. Folk want a fine excuse to get boozed. You'll make a pretty penny out of it.

LANCASTER. That's enough of that, Sarah Hardacre, and you're all wrong. I'm giving a barrel of beer.

SARAH. Givin'?

LANCASTER. Aye. Givin'.

SARAH. That's something fresh. You usually throw your money around like a man with no arms.

LANCASTER. I'm not daft wi' *my* brass. Anyway, that's what I'm prepared to do. What about thee? He's your son.

SARAH. What about me?

LANCASTER. Well, if I give the beer, least you can do is to make a tater pie.

SARAH. What! For the whole street?

LANCASTER. I'm givin' the beer, aren't I?

SARAH. Sprat to catch a mackerel.

LANCASTER. Eh?

SARAH. D'you think I'm that daft? They'll have supped a barrel in no time, then they'll want more, and then there'll be no gettin' into the "Flyin' Shuttle". And I suppose you'd like plenty of salt put in the pie, eh?

LANCASTER. Live and let live. Well, will you make the pie?

SARAH. I've enough to do as it is.

LANCASTER. If you're thinking of the cost, you needn't worry. I'll find the brass.

SARAH. How's your brass going to get over the rationing?

LANCASTER. You leave that to me.

SARAH. I ought to give you in charge for black marketeering.

LANCASTER. I tell you we want to show our appreciation to Jack. (*He peers into the dish, then looks at* SARAH *hintingly*.) What about that bit left in the dish, lass?

SARAH. You've had your whack. There's another day, remember.

LANCASTER. Go on, Sarah, just a spoonful of gravy to sop up my bread.

SARAH. Aye, and it will be a spoonful an' all. (*She gives him another helping.*) Doesn't that housekeeper of yours ever feed you?

LANCASTER. Not on grub like this, she doesn't. When it's not in 'em, it's not in 'em. . . . I suppose now that Jack's back he'll start thinking about it.

SARAH. Now what are you on about?

LANCASTER. Your Jack, settling down.

SARAH. Maybe.

LANCASTER. Be kind of lonely here for you on your own when he's wed, won't it, lass?

SARAH. A woman's little time for company when she's got a house on her hands. Particularly here with everlasting muck everywhere.

LANCASTER. Aye, 'tis mucky here, but there's other places that aren't quite so mucky. And I've had an eye-opener since the war.

SARAH. Now what are you chunnering about?

LANCASTER. Listen, I'll tell you. (*He moves bread board away to* L.) All these south-country folk who've been sent up here to work— the way they chuck their money about! Eh! A pub down there after the war. (*He pauses.*) D'you fancy it, lass?

SARAH. Just a minute, Harry Lancaster. Are you asking me to marry thee?

LANCASTER. You can put it that way if you like.

SARAH. Not if you were the last man on earth.

LANCASTER. If I was, I'd have no time proposing—I'd be kept too busy.

SARAH. Oh-ho! Don't flatter yourself . . . you're past all that.

LANCASTER. Maybe. But they'd have to put up with me. I'd be the best man alive. An' it'd be very interestin'. What about it, lass?

SARAH (*after a pause*). H'm.

LANCASTER. What d'you mean—h'm?

SARAH. Who'd wear the trousers?

LANCASTER. Nay, lass. We'd come to an arrangement. Ah! I can just see it now—a pub in country down south, with a pull in for motor coaches, a proper restaurant noted for thy cooking. . . . We'd coin it, Sarah. We'd coin it. Can't you see?

SARAH. Aye, I can see me sweating in the kitchen, morning noon and night, while you're standing on the doorstep with a belly on you twice the size it is now. No, thank you!

LANCASTER. Nay, lass—I'd get you servants.

SARAH. There you go! *You'd* get me servants. . . ! Let me tell you, Harry Lancaster——

LANCASTER. All right! All right! We'll have no arguments. You hold the purse strings.

SARAH. You bet your life I would.

LANCASTER. What do you say, then?

SARAH. Same as I said before. Nothing doing.

LANCASTER. Think well, lass. I'm in no hurry.

SARAH. No more am I.

LANCASTER. I've a tidy pile saved up.

SARAH. By gum, you ought to have. That husband o' mine pushed a fortune across your counter.

LANCASTER. He was a lucky man to have had you for a wife, was John Hardacre. What a fool he was! By gum, what a fool!

SARAH. Don't you call John Hardacre a fool.

LANCASTER. You called him worse than that when he was alive.

SARAH. I was his wife.

LANCASTER. Ay. And I wish you were mine.

SARAH. That'll be quite enough for one evening. Come on. Let's be seeing the back side of you. Come on. (*She rises, moves below the table and starts to clear it.*)

(LANCASTER *rises, moves* L. *of the table and picks up his hat.*)

LANCASTER. We'll leave it like that, then, eh, Sarah?

SARAH. Like what?

LANCASTER. You'll make the pies for the do?

SARAH. Maybe. We'll see.

LANCASTER. And as for the other little matter. . . ?

SARAH (*crossing to the fire with the hot-pot*). You're wasting your time.

LANCASTER (*moving to the door up* L. C.). There's no hurry, lass. I've had it in my mind long enough. Just think it over and take your time. (*He opens the door.*)

SARAH (*picking up a plate*). See this?

LANCASTER (*turning*). Aye. One of your best plates.

SARAH. If you aren't on the other side of that door in just one second, you get it at your head. (*She makes a movement as though to throw the plate.*)

LANCASTER. Nay, Sarah, your best service?

(*He goes out pulling the door to.*)

SARAH (*crossing above the table to* R. *and turning*). That fooled him.

(LANCASTER *opens the door.*)

LANCASTER (*halfway in*). Once I've set my mind on a thing, I never give up.

(SARAH *flings the plate. The door slams. The plate shatters against it.* SARAH *screams, then crosses and picks up the pieces.*)

SARAH. My best china! And not even my husband.

QUICK CURTAIN

ACT II

SCENE: *The Private Bar of the "Flying Shuttle". Later the same evening.*

> *There is a short counter down* L. *with a stool near each end of it.
> A partition, with a door in it slightly* R. *of* C., *runs across from the top
> of the counter to the* R. *wall and divides the Private from the Public Bar
> behind. Between the door and the counter there is a long bench or settle.
> Behind the counter are two dressers whose shelves are filled with bottles
> and glasses, and a cash register. In the Public Bar there is a short counter,
> supposedly a continuation of the one visible in the Private Bar; a table
> and a chest-of-drawers with a radio on it. Downstage* R. *a door leads
> into the street and when it is open a brick wall can be seen.*
> *(See the Ground Plan and Photograph of Scene.)*

> *When the* CURTAIN *rises most of the patrons of this very small room
> can be heard behind the partition in the Public Bar where a dart match
> is in progress. Only* MRS. DORBELL, *a beshawled old crone, is in the
> Private Bar. She is sitting on the upstage stool at the counter, regarding
> with a melancholy expression the remains of her drink. Obviously she
> is weary of the loneliness and longing for company. The* BARMAID *is up-
> stage above the partition.*

1st VOICE (*in Public Bar*). Your turn now.
2nd VOICE. I know that. (*He throws the dart.*)
3rd VOICE. That's a double six, Bill.
4th VOICE. Double six.

> (*The* BARMAID *moves downstage behind the counter.*)

BARMAID. Did you call, Mrs. Dorbell?
MRS. DORBELL. No, I didn't.
BARMAID. Have you finished your drink?
MRS. DORBELL. No, I haven't, not yet.

(*The* BARMAID *moves upstage.* HARRY LANCASTER *enters down* R. *He
crosses to the counter, humming, and gets apron from peg on wall downstage of counter.*)

LANCASTER. Good evening, Mrs. Dorbell.
MRS. DORBELL. Good evening.
LANCASTER. You don't look so pleased.
MRS. DORBELL. What can you expect, sitting here all alone
with all of 'em gone in there?

LANCASTER. There's nowt to stop you from going in there with
'em.

MRS. DORBELL. Darts! I don't want no darts in my eye. An'
what have you been up to? You look very pleased with yourself.

LANCASTER. Them as asks no questions gets no lies told. (*He
hums again and crosses to the door* C.)

(*Enter* MRS. JENKINS *and* JANEY *down* R.)

(*Turning at the door.*) Good evening, Mrs. Jenkins.

MRS. JENKINS. Good evening.

LANCASTER. And you too, Janey.

JANEY. Good evening.

LANCASTER. Don't often see you here.

JANEY. No.

MRS. JENKINS (*pausing to listen to the voices from the other bar*). No,
my daughter receives 'er guests in the privacy of 'er 'ome. Our
kitchen's full of 'em sometimes.

LANCASTER. Is it? Doesn't seem to empty my pub. (*He looks
through the door.*) Public Bar doing nicely to-night, with the dart
match.

(*A dart is thrown. Several voices can be heard saying, "Good, good!" "Good
shot!" "That's champion!" etc.*)

(*As he goes into the Public Bar.*) Good shot, Jack, lad.

(*He exits and goes behind the counter upstage.* MRS. JENKINS *and* JANEY
move up C. *to the door and peep through.* MRS. DORBELL *cranes round
the corner end of the screen.*)

MRS. JENKINS. Yes, he *is* here.

JANEY. It's him all right. He's come with her, that's what he's
done.

MRS. JENKINS. First night home. Starting well, isn't he? Not even
been across to see you.

JANEY. It's her all right. Why doesn't she stick to Joe Truman?

MRS. JENKINS (*crossing to the counter*). And all them foreign troops.
Don't talk to me about them. I'll have a bitter, Mr. Lancaster.
(*She taps on the counter.*)

MRS. DORBELL. Well, you'll never hear me say a wrong word
agen 'em. Not been the same woman, I 'aven't, not since they've
gone.

(LANCASTER *comes downstage and puts a glass on the counter.*)

MRS. JENKINS. English born and bred, that's me. (*She pays.*)

(LANCASTER *puts the money in the till and moves upstage.*)

MRS. DORBELL. Used to put their money on the counter and
leave it there. The soul o' generosity they were. God bless 'em,
wherever they are.

(JANEY *opens the door* C.)

MRS. JENKINS. An Englishman's good enough for my daughter, isn't he, Janey? (*She moves to the* L. *end of the bench with her drink.*)

A VOICE (*in the Public Bar*). It's me now.

JANEY. Yes, Ma. Shall we go in and watch the darts?

MRS. JENKINS. You stay where you are.

JANEY. But she's in there with him.

MRS. JENKINS (*sitting on the bench,* L. *end*). Let 'im come looking for you.

JANEY (*sitting on the bench,* R. *end*). I know. But I didn't put my best on, let alone get my hair set, just to sit 'ere with two ladies.

MRS. JENKINS. Now, our Janey. You heard what your mother said. She's not got what you've got. *And*—you've never been out with them foreigners for what you could get out of them.

MRS. DORBELL. They never got anything out of me, neither.

MRS. JENKINS. Well, I can't say as they've missed much. (*She drinks.*)

MRS. DORBELL. I've not always been as old as I am, Ma Jenkins. When I was young, I was there when they were dishing it out.

(MRS. JENKINS *sniggers.* LANCASTER *comes downstage behind the counter.*) And you can go to the devil.

LANCASTER. Ladies, ladies——! (*He takes a notebook and pencil from the downstage dresser and then leans over the counter and does his accounts.*)

MRS. DORBELL. Her and her daughter! Funny thing to me she was never called up.

MRS. JENKINS. My daughter's on war work. Aren't you, Janey?

JANEY. And I'm not the foreman's pet either, like somebody I know.

MRS. DORBELL. And I won't hear a word said about Joe Truman, either.

MRS. JENKINS. Why don't you ask *him* why *he* wasn't called up? Jack Hardacre didn't wait to be called; he volunteered. A 'ero, that's what 'e is, a 'ero. (*She drinks.*)

MRS. DORBELL. There might have been method in his madness. I notice he isn't volunteering to come in here.

LANCASTER. If this here bickering doesn't stop—(*A dart is thrown in the Public Bar*)—I'll be asking somebody to volunteer to clear off out of here.

1st VOICE (*in the Public Bar*). Sixty-nine left, Milly.

2nd VOICE. Are you trying for bung-hole, Milly?

3rd VOICE. Go on, Milly, have a do!

JACK'S VOICE. Treble nineteen and double six, Milly love. You can't miss.

JANEY. Hear that, Ma? He called her love.

MRS. JENKINS. It's only a game.

MRS. DORBELL. Ha!

MRS. JENKINS. What d'you mean, "ha"?

MRS. DORBELL. Thinkin'. Have I got to ask if I can laugh at my own thoughts now?

MRS. JENKINS. I'd like to know what you was thinkin'.

MRS. DORBELL. I'll bet you would. An' I bet you have got a pretty good idea.

MRS. JENKINS. You old besom, you. All you're fit for is sitting there waiting for somebody to come in and buy you a drink.

LANCASTER. That's enough. One of you in the Public Bar, or all outside.

MRS. JENKINS. It's true what I say. Never even seen her buy herself a drink yet.

MRS. DORBELL. Well, if they want to buy me. . . .

LANCASTER. Come thee on, Mrs. Dorbell, for the sake of peace.

MRS. DORBELL. Oh, it's me you're turning out, is it, Harry Lancaster?

LANCASTER. Aye, for the sake of peace.

MRS. DORBELL. Seventy-seven I am, and worked every day of my life since I can remember. Alone I am, and only ten bob a week apart from the extra shillings they gie at the Public Assistance and what I can get for my clothing coupons. Nobody'll gie me a job. They say I'm too old. When I was working and had it, I spent it wi' thee, Harry. Now I'm past it, it's as she says, I've to sit here waitin' for anybody with a kind heart to buy an old woman a drink. And bless 'em all, there's many of 'em. Many an' many a time I've sat here dyin' for a swig and not darin' to finish off the bottom of the glass, because it meant going home to an empty grate an' nothin' to eat in the house. Starved to death I would ha' done in this war, if it hadn't ha' been for Mrs. Hardacre's British Restaurant.

MRS. JENKINS. He, he!

(*There are general crowd noises in the Public Bar.*)

MRS. DORBELL. And gallons o' Guinness, too, them Yankee and Canadian lads bought me.

MRS. JENKINS. Oh, Canadians.

MRS. DORBELL. Yes, and three of 'em came to my house to see how I was livin'. Cried, one of 'em did, drunk as he was. . . . And every night I get down on my bendeds and say my prayers for 'em wherever they are. (*She rises.*)

MRS. JENKINS. Oh, prayers now.

MRS. DORBELL (*moving to* MRS. JENKINS). But you, Ma Jenkins, though I can't afford it till this here Beveridge Report comes in, I tell you I'd sing in the blooming gutter for my drink afore I'd take one from thee.

LANCASTER. Come, come, Mrs. Dorbell. . . .

MRS. DORBELL (*moving to* LANCASTER). All right, Harry Lancaster, I'll go into the next room and I'll bet I'll not be short of a drink there. Christian country! Ha!

MRS. JENKINS. If it wasn't a Christian country. . . .

MRS. DORBELL. It's the likes o' you. . . . Give 'em ten bob a week and let 'em die . . . so long as they die in a room alone, botherin' nobody. Well, let me die in a pub holding a glass. (*Crossing to* R. C.) An' all I hope is, I've got the blooming strength to drain it *afore* I kick the bucket.

(*She exits into the Public Bar.* LANCASTER *moves upstage.*)

MRS. JENKINS. Tch. Tch. Dirty old faggot. Me buy her a drink! Ha! That'll be the day.

LANCASTER (*putting a glass on the Public Bar counter*). Here you are, Mrs. Dorbell. You forgot your Guinness.

MRS. DORBELL'S VOICE. Aye, bless you, lad.

LANCASTER. Don't bless me. I never give nowt away. Them as left it for you wanted no names mentionin'.

MRS. DORBELL'S VOICE. Bless 'em all the same, whoever it was.

JACK'S VOICE. Well done, Walter, well done!

MILLY'S VOICE. Ooh! Good shot, good shot!

JANEY (*rising and looking through the door* C.). I wish he'd come in here, Ma.

MRS. JENKINS. A fine thing it is, having to chase him.

JANEY (*crossing down* R.). Why couldn't he have come over to our house as soon as he'd seen his Ma?

MRS. JENKINS. Don't waste time crying. He isn't here to see you. And when you do cry watch that your eye black doesn't run all down your face.

JANEY (*crossing to* R. *of the bench*). When he does come round, you *will* go out and leave us alone, won't you, Ma?

MRS. JENKINS. Don't you fret yourself about that. I'll just give him until I've supped this, and if he isn't here then, *I'm* going to fetch him.

JANEY (*looking through the door*). Go on, Ma, hurry up and drink it.

MRS. JENKINS. I'm choking myself for nobody.

JANEY. Oh, go on, Ma. I'll get you another. (*She crosses to the counter.*) What'll you have?

MRS. JENKINS. Bitter, I'll 'ave. (*She rises, moves to the counter above* JANEY *and puts her glass down.*) And I'll want an excuse, so as it won't look as though I'm going in there on purpose. Lend me a penny.

(JANEY *gives* MRS. JENKINS *a penny.* MRS. JENKINS *crosses to the door* C. *and exits into the Public Bar.*)

JANEY (*knocking on the counter*). Bitter, please.

LANCASTER (*coming downstage*). Anything for yourself?

JANEY. I don't drink. (*She moves to the* L. *end of the bench.*)

JACK'S VOICE. Oh! Milly, love, that's brilliant.

MILLY'S VOICE. What's the score now?

JACK'S VOICE. Hullo, Joe Truman, what's up wi' thee, lad? You don't look as though you're having any luck.

(JOE TRUMAN *enters* C. *from the Public Bar.*)

JOE (*entering*). Leave me be. Leave me be, can't you?

MRS. DORBELL'S VOICE. Never you mind, Joe. Lucky in love, unlucky in t'other things.

JOE. Put a sock in it, Ma Dorbell. (*He shuts the door and crosses to counter up* L.) Wish folk'd let me alone. Hey there, Harry. Give us a double. Row that side gives me the bloody pip. (*He puts some money on the counter.*)

LANCASTER. Now then, guard that tongue, Joe Truman. You're not in the Public Bar now, you know. (*He pours the double and puts it on the counter; takes the money and puts it in the till.*)

JOE (*glancing at* JANEY). There's nobody in except her, 'n she hears worse from me in t'factory when I catch her dawdling about on her job.

JANEY (*sitting on the bench* L. *end*). Who d'you think you're talking about, Joe Truman?

JOE. I dunno, the ticket's fell off.

JANEY (*rising and moving to* JOE). I'll stand no insults from you, Joe Truman.

JOE. Well, sit to 'em, then.

JANEY. You wouldn't dare to let Jack Hardacre hear you talking to me like that.

JOE. I wouldn't, wouldn't I? What's he got to do with it?

JANEY. Just let him hear you, that's all. He'd paralyse you. He's my intended, and don't you forget it. (*She moves to the bench and sits.*)

JOE. His intentions seem to have changed, if you ask me.

JANEY (*turning*). What do you mean?

JOE. You've got eyes. Go in there and see. Ask Milly Southern what *she* thinks about it.

JANEY. You wouldn't say that to his face.

JOE. That's what you think.

JANEY. I dare you to.

JOE. Let him come in here, I will.

LANCASTER. Now that'll be quite enough o' that, see. You ought to have more sense, man. Sup up that double and get home. It's sleep you want. Now come on, lad, be sensible. When you look for trouble with Jack Hardacre you're sticking your neck out with a champion boxer. And the factory won't pay you no wages while you're in the hospital.

JOE (*drinking*). Go in there, I'm not wanted, come in here, I'm not wanted.

LANCASTER. Aye, that's right, now you're talking sense—you're not wanted, see.

JOE (*putting his glass on the counter*). All right, Harry Lancaster, I'll get my skates on and go home.

(*He crosses down* R. *and exits.*)

LANCASTER. What have you been doing to him?

JANEY. Who? Joe Truman?

LANCASTER. Aye.

JANEY. I don't have anything to do with *him*. You want to ask *her* in there.

LANCASTER. How do you know it's *her* he's after?

JANEY. H'm.

LANCASTER. After all, when a girl lets it be known she's already engaged——

JANEY. Do you mean to say. . . . He's never. . . . (*She checks herself.*) I don't care for Joe Truman.

LANCASTER. It's nothing to do with me. I was wonderin', that's all. Moanin' and groanin', sighin' and shiftin'. Hard lines on a fellow when he's got it that bad.

JANEY. D'you mean to say that's why he's. . . . Blimey!

LANCASTER. I'm meanin' to say nowt.

(*A silence falls.* JANEY *sighs.*)

MILLY'S VOICE. Oh, Jack, ducky!

(*General voices in the Public Bar.*)

JANEY. "Ducky!" (*She rises and moves to the counter.*) I think I'll have a drink. (*She sits on the upstage stool.*)

LANCASTER. What'll it be?

JANEY. Small port.

(LANCASTER *pours out the port and places the glass on the counter.*)

LANCASTER. Do you think you ought to let Jack Hardacre see you drinkin'?

JANEY. I can please myself if I want to, can't I?

LANCASTER. 'Course you can. Some fellows like to see a bit of spirit in a girl.

JANEY. Um?

LANCASTER. Some don't.

JANEY. Who d'you mean?

LANCASTER. Oh, some fellers. A feller in my position can't take sides. All the same, I see a lot, and I can do my own thinkin'.

1st VOICE (*in the Public Bar*). Give us a bitter, Rosie.

2nd VOICE. By gum, wharra match!

(LANCASTER *moves upstage and serves beer in the Public Bar.* MRS. JENKINS *enters* C.)

MRS. JENKINS (*crossing to* JANEY). He's comin'. Didn't know we were here, he says. (*She arranges* JANEY's *dress.*)

JANEY (*getting down from the stool*). Don't muck about with me, Ma, I've been mucked about too much already.

(LANCASTER *comes downstage.*)

MRS. JENKINS. Now, our Janey, you want to look your best, don't you? He hasn't seen you for three years, remember.

LANCASTER (*putting a glass of bitter on the counter*). Small port and a bitter, that'll be three and sevenpence.

MRS. JENKINS. Our Janey—you're drinkin'! (*She puts money on the counter.*)

JANEY. I can please myself, can't I?

(LANCASTER *puts the money in the till.*)

MRS. JENKINS. Of course, if you won't take your Ma's advice. What'll he be thinkin' if he sees you?

JANEY (*crossing with her port to the door* c.). She's drinkin'.

MRS. JENKINS (*moving, with her glass, to the bench*). Ginger ale. Blown up wi' wind she'll be. (*She gets* L. *of the bench.*) But go on, make a proper muck of it. Don't take any notice of me. If you'd play your cards well you could be Mrs. Hardacre before he goes back. Sergeant's wife's pay, no factory work, and that bullyin' Ma of his wouldn't get a penny. Her and her British Restaurant!

JANEY. Why did he have to take Milly Southern to that dart match before he came to see me? (*She sits on the bench,* R. *end.*)

MRS. JENKINS. Go on, dafty. Give him time to get used to being at home. Besides, if there were twenty thousand hers, you'd still have *that*. (*She points to the engagement ring.*) Anyway, sup that down before he comes in and forget about her in there. Don't know why she doesn't get wed to Joe Truman if you say he's so sweet on her.

JANEY. Maybe it isn't her he's after. She's not the only lass in Salford.

MRS. JENKINS. Maybe it isn't then, what does it matter?

LANCASTER (*singing*). Diver beware, diver take care, danger is near, so beware, beware.

A VOICE (*in the Public Bar*). Where you off to, Jack?

(*General voices in the Public Bar.*)

JACK'S VOICE. I'm just going in there. Back directly.

MRS. JENKINS. Here he is. (*She takes the port from* JANEY.) He mustn't see this. (*She rises and crosses to the counter, leaving her bag on the bench.*) Well, it won't be wasted. (*She pours* JANEY'S *drink into her own.*)

JANEY (*rising*). Go on, Ma, you hoppit.

(*Enter* JACK *from the Public Bar. He stands by the door* c.)

JACK. Oh, hello there, Janey! There you are, then.

JANEY. Yes, I'm here. Though you mightn't have thought so, the notice that's bein' taken of me.

JACK. I've been playing in t'dart match.

JANEY. I've got ears.

JACK. Yes, a very good game it is, too.

JANEY. Is it?

JACK. Yes, very good. Shall I bring you a drink, Janey?

JANEY. And I see you've forgotten I don't drink.

JACK. Give me a chance to get home, Janey. I've almost forgotten what England's like. (*To* MRS. JENKINS.) Will you have a drink, Mrs. Jenkins?

MRS. JENKINS. "Mrs. . . . ." Listen to him! "Mrs. Jenkins!" Go on with you, Jack. You can call me Ma. I'll have a bitter. Go on, Janey, Jack's asked you to have a drink. Give her a port, Jack. She doesn't drink, you know. Just to celebrate, you understand.

JACK. Wheel 'em in, Harry. (*Crossing down* R.) Bitter and a small port.

MRS. JENKINS. What about thee, Jack?

JACK. I've got one in there.

JANEY. Well, go and fetch it here.

MRS. JENKINS (*crossing to* JACK). No, no, Jack. You stay where you are.

JACK. No, don't leave us alone.

MRS. JENKINS. I'll bring it for you.

JACK (*preventing her going*). Don't leave us alone. (*He moves up* R. C.) Janey being so upset and all. I tell you what—why don't we all go in there and join in the fun with everybody else?

(MRS. JENKINS *drops down* R.)

JANEY. Me go in there? I shouldn't ha' thought bein' in here wasn't private enough.

JACK. Well, I *am* playin' in the match, Janey. Won't you come in and watch?

JANEY. But you've just come 'ome.

JACK. I know I've just come 'ome.

JANEY. And all you want me to do is go in there and watch you playin' darts.

JACK. What's wrong wi' darts? It's a very good game.

JANEY. We used to know a better.

MRS. JENKINS. Yes, why don't you slip across to our house, there's nobody in.

LANCASTER (*putting glasses on the counter*). Port and bitter, Jack.

JACK (*crossing to the counter*). Aye, thank you, Harry.

LANCASTER. That'll be three and sevenpence.

JANEY (*motioning* MRS. JENKINS *to clear off into the other bar and crossing to the door* C.). Mrs. Dorbell's waitin' in there for you, Ma.

MRS. JENKINS (*crossing to the counter*). Still the same Janey she is, Jack, same now as when you went away.

JACK (*handing* MRS. JENKINS *the bitter*). Is she? (*He crosses to* C. *with the port.*)

MRS. JENKINS. She is, an' all.

JACK. Small port for you, Janey.

JANEY (*moving above the table to* C.). Thank you, love. (*She sits on the bench.*)

MRS. JENKINS (*dropping down* L.). Always kept herself to herself, she has, all the time.

JACK (*moving back to the counter, upstage end*). I thought as much. Three and sevenpence. (*He pays.*)

(LANCASTER *puts the money in the till and goes upstage.* JANEY *rises, leaves her handbag on the bench, crosses to* JACK *and puts her arms round him.*)

Hello.

JANEY. Oh, come on, love.

(*She pulls* JACK *down on to the bench,* L. *end.*)

JACK (*sighing heavily*). It is grand to be back.

JANEY. Yes, it is, isn't it? Do you think I've changed, Jack? (*She runs her hand up and down his arm, and puts her head on his shoulder.*)

JACK. No, not a bit.

JANEY. Well, aren't you glad I haven't changed?

MRS. JENKINS. There's not many round here like our Janey.

JANEY. Here's your handbag, Ma. (*She picks it up off the bench.*)

MRS. JENKINS (*crossing to* JANEY *and taking the bag*). I suppose I'd better be off. Mrs. Dorbell's waitin' in there for me. . . . (*She crosses to the door* C.) . . . and leave you two love birds alone.

(*She goes out into the Public Bar.*)

JANEY. Love birds, Jack, love birds.

JACK. Oh, you and me.

JANEY. Aye.

JACK. Oh, lovely.

JANEY. Didn't you bring me anything home?

JACK. Oh aye, I forgot.

JANEY (*eagerly*). Did you really, Jack?

JACK. Aye, it's—er——

JANEY (*jealously*). That Milly Southern hasn't seen it, has she? She didn't get her fingers on it, did she?

JACK. I don't suppose she'd want it.

JANEY. What is it?

JACK. Well—it's—er—some stuff for your finger-ends, lipstick and that tack. Oh, and some silk stockings.

JANEY. Where is it, Jack?

JACK. At our house. I'll be letting you have it.

JANEY. Thank you, Jack. (*She sits on his knee.*) Jack, it makes me go all funny inside to have you near me again.

JACK. Does it?

JANEY. Don't you feel funny like?

JACK. Not 'arf. It's gettin' warm in 'ere, isn't it, proper warm.

JANEY. I should ha' thought you'd ha' been used to where it's warm.

JACK. What d'you mean, Janey?

JANEY. From what I've heard other fellows say who've come home, it was warm enough there when they went on leave.

JACK. Do you mean the desert?

JANEY. Funny sort o' desert, with all them black girls dressed in trousers made o' butter muslin.

JACK. There was none o' them billeted near us.

JANEY. What were the girls there like, then?

JACK. Same as girls here, I suppose.

JANEY. Did you go out with any? (*She gets off his knee.*)

JACK. You need money in your purse for that kind of racket. We're in t' British Army, remember.

JANEY. I was always thinkin' o' you, Jack. Did you think o' me?

JACK. Aye, many a time.

JANEY (*giggling*). What was you thinkin'?

JACK. Oh, I was wonderin', you know, hopin'.

JANEY. Hopin' what?

JACK. Hopin' you was happy.

(JANEY *smiles and puts* JACK's *arm round her waist.* JACK *pulls his arm away.* JANEY *pulls it back.*)

JANEY. I wrote you, didn't I?

JACK. Yes, you did.

JANEY. And didn't you like my letters?

JACK. Very nice writing.

JANEY. Are you happy, Jack? (*She lies across* JACK's *knees and runs her hand down his leg twice.*)

(JACK *scratches his leg.*)

JACK. I'm all right.

(JANEY's *hair is tickling* JACK's *nose. He makes a movement.*)

JANEY (*raising her head*). What's the matter?

JACK. Just thinkin'.

JANEY. What about?

JACK. Oh, nothin'.

JANEY. Aren't you glad to be home?

JACK. Aye.

JANEY. When're you goin' back?

JACK (*rising and turning on her*). Dammit, I'm here, aren't I?

JANEY (*rising*). You've got no need to snap at me.

JACK. Well, all the lads are fed to the teeth, they are, with bein' asked, "When're you goin' back?" before any of 'em have dropped their packs. Suppose we started to ask you civvies when you were goin' to join up?

(CHARLIE FOX *opens the door* C. *and puts his head into the bar.* MUNTER *also puts his head round the door.*)

MILLY (*in the Public Bar*). Your shot coming up, Jack.

MUNTER. Time's up, Jack, you're wanted this side.

JANEY. You get out, Ted Munter. (*To* JACK.) And look here you, we can't all be in uniform, and there's others besides me, remember, and them as don't come from these parts. (*She jerks her thumb towards the other bar.*) That Bevin Beauty your Ma's got staying in her house. I don't think it's right she should be sleepin' there while you're home.

JACK. Do you mean Milly?

JANEY. Milly! Oh, it's Milly already, is it?

JACK. Milly's her name, isn't it?

JANEY. Well, Joe Truman won't like it.

JACK. Oh, he won't, won't he?

JANEY. His pet at the factory, she is.

JACK. Oh, she is, is she? Joe Truman, eh? Somebody else on work of National Importance.

JANEY. Well, somebody's got to do the work.

JACK. The work I'm thinkin' of isn't work.

JANEY. What do you mean, Jack Hardacre?

(MRS. JENKINS *enters* C. CHARLIE *crosses to the counter.*)

JACK. And from what I've been hearin' there's a lot of that been goin' on lately.

JANEY. If you're meanin' me, I'll have you know that I kept myself to myself, and it wasn't for the want of chances either.

MRS. JENKINS. What's all this? What's the matter?

CHARLIE (*sitting on the counter*). Is there a row on?

MUNTER (*coming down* R.). Come on, Jack lad, it'll soon be closing time.

(MRS. DORBELL *enters* C. *She stands* R. *of the door.*)

JACK. And you keep out of this, all of you, leave us alone.

JANEY. I don't know what's come over you.

MRS. JENKINS. There's a big change in you, Jack Hardacre, a big change indeed.

JACK (*crossing* JANEY *to* C.; *to* MRS. JENKINS). Now listen. (*He embraces them all.*) Listen. I've just come home. Stood all the way in the train from London. Stood, d'you hear? Stood in t' corridor watching Jerry prisoners sitting comfortable in a reserved compartment. I've just dropped my pack, see? An' I'm enjoyin' myself in there, see?—enjoyin' myself. An' I know I've changed, Mrs. Jenkins. Twenty-odd when I joined up—and that Jack Hardacre that left this street is never coming back, never.

(JANEY *sits on the bench,* L. *end.* LANCASTER *enters* C.)

LANCASTER (*coming between* MRS. DORBELL *and* MRS. JENKINS). Come on, Jack.

JACK. I'm on me way.

LANCASTER. And you too, Mrs. Dorbell, out of it. Trust you to be where there's an argument.

(*The* BARMAID *comes downstage behind the counter.*)

MRS. DORBELL. At me again! Oh, you go to the devil.

BARMAID (*to* CHARLIE). Eh, eh! That's a polished top, get off it.

LANCASTER (*crossing to the counter; to* CHARLIE). Eh, what do you think this is, a blooming grand stand? Get down, will you, get down off the counter! Come on, Jack, lad. You're holdin' up the game. (*He pushes* CHARLIE *off the counter.*)

JACK (*crossing to the door* C.). I'm on my way, I tell you.

MUNTER (*moving up to* JACK). Come on, Jack, put a jerk in it, you only want. . . .

JACK (*shaking* MUNTER *off*). Gie over pawin' me. I'm comin', I've told you. I'm comin'. And listen, everybody. (*Turning; deliberately.*) Listen, all of you, I wish to issue the following warning. If anybody else asks me when I'm going back, I'll knock his blooming block off, male or female. (*He turns into the Public Bar.*) Give me my darts.

(JACK *exits into the Public Bar. He is followed by* MUNTER, MRS. DORBELL, CHARLIE *and* LANCASTER. *The* BARMAID *moves upstage.*)

A VOICE (*in the Public Bar*). Here you are, Jack lad. Here's your arrows, forty-eight you want.

MILLY'S VOICE. You'll only need two darts, Jack.

MUNTER'S VOICE. The old favourite, Jack, eight and double top.

A VOICE. Bung 'em in, lad.

MRS. JENKINS (*shutting the door*). What's happened? What've you been doin'?

JANEY (*rising and taking a step away to* L. C.). Leave me alone.

MRS. JENKINS. Don't be a fool. Hurry and sup up and get into the other bar with you.

JANEY. That's just what she'd like me to do.

MRS. JENKINS (*contemptuously*). Her!

JANEY (*buttoning up her coat*). Yes, her! She'd like to see me chasin' him while she's in there. Well, she won't, see? She won't. I've got him, and I won't let him go. (*She moves to the bench, picks up her bag and crosses to the door down* R.) Let him try to wriggle out if he can, just let him try . . . that's all!

(*She exits.*)

CURTAIN

SCENE: MRS. HARDACRE'S *kitchen-living-room. Two weeks later. Evening.*

The sofa is now made up as a bed. On it is the armchair from down R.; *also* MILLY'S *overcoat and a book. The three chairs which were round the table are now on it and the table has been pushed up towards the sofa.* MILLY'S *skirt is over the back of the chair above the fire and her shoes are beneath it. The clothes horse still carries some of her underclothing.*

When the CURTAIN *rises* JACK *is sitting in the easy chair.* SARAH *is at the chest-of-drawers.*

SARAH. Well, I shall be glad when this war is over, and I've finished with the British Restaurant and get me housework done at a respectable hour, and not be at it until this time every night. I thought you were going to pack your things.

JACK. Oh, leave me be, Ma. I will when I can get in the bedroom. Milly hasn't finished upstairs.

SARAH (*crossing to the sofa*). She's taking her time, too.

JACK. Well, she can't change down here, can she?

SARAH. Here, help me with the chair, love.

JACK (*rising and crossing up* R.). It's bad enough making her sleep on the sofa so that I can have the bedroom.

(SARAH *and* JACK *bring the armchair to its place down* R.)

I wish I knew where she's going to-night.

SARAH. You can easily find out if you ask her. (*She moves up to* R. *of the table.*) Table, love.

(JACK *crosses to* L., *turns, moves in to* L. *of the table and helps* SARAH *to bring it downstage.*)

SARAH. Well, I don't know. I should have thought you would have had enough on your hands with the other one. Is she coming round to-night?

(*They put the chairs round the table.*)

JACK. I suppose so. (*He drops into the chair above the table.*)

SARAH (*putting the tablecloth on*). When do you get your next leave? (*She moves down* R. *to the armchair and sits.*)

JACK. I can come round every night till eleven if I want to.

SARAH. You sound as though you don't care whether you come home or not.

(*There is a knock on the door up* L. C.)

JACK. Um.
SARAH (*rising*). This'll be her.

(*She exits down* R.)

JACK. Come in. (*He rises.*)

(*Enter* JANEY. *She is wearing bright-coloured slacks.*)

JANEY. Hullo! Hope you didn't think I wasn't coming. (*She comes down* L. *of the table.*)
JACK. Sit down.
JANEY (*pulling out the chair* L. *of the table*). You aren't dressed yet.

(*Enter* SARAH *dragging the bath.*)

SARAH (*putting the bath down below the* R. *end of the table*). He's going to have a bath, and I'm just getting it ready.

(*She goes out down* R.)

JACK. Milly hasn't finished changing up there yet, you see.
JANEY (*sitting on the table,* L. *end*). Is she going out?
JACK. Of course she is—I'm going to have a bath, aren't I? (*He indicates the underclothes on the clothes-horse.*) Those're her things.
JANEY (*getting off the table and moving to the easy chair*). Yes, I didn't think they were your Ma's. (*She sits.*)
JACK. Airing 'em.
JANEY. H'm. Think you're going out with her?
JACK. I'm going to have a bath, aren't I? (*He moves down* L. *of the table.*)
JANEY. Where're we going.
JACK. I dunno, I've got to pack my kit.
JANEY. Pack your kit! Can't you do that later?
JACK. No, I can't. I don't want to be all of a rush in the morning.
JANEY. You've no need to snap at me.
JACK. I'm not snapping at you, I'm only telling you.
JANEY. Like my trousers? (*She rises and crosses to* R. *below the table.*)
JACK. Aye, they're all right.
JANEY. Fashionable, they are.
JACK. Are they?
JANEY. The man said it was the only pair he had in the shop. (*She crosses back to the easy chair and sits on the arm.*)
JACK. That's lucky.
JANEY. Aren't you going to kiss me?
JACK. Don't be daft; Ma's in there.
JANEY. If you'd come to our house, my Ma would have gone out, like she always used to do.

JACK. I know all about that. (*He moves below the table, picks up the bath and crosses with it to the fireplace.*)

(JANEY *rises and pulls the facecloth out of the bath.*)

(*He throws the facecloth back into the bath.*) And another thing—I don't want anybody to rub me down when I'm having a bath. And as for your trousers, I can't say I'm interested in women's clothes.

(*He sits in the easy chair and stares in front of him.*)

JANEY (*crossing to* R. *above the table*). Well, you seem to be interested enough in her underclothes. You've done nothing but gawp at them since I've been here.

JACK. I wasn't gawping. I was only thinking.

JANEY (*coming down* R. *and moving below the table*). I bet she left 'em there on purpose.

JACK. They've got to be aired, haven't they?

JANEY. She could have aired them when you weren't in the house.

JACK. Well, she didn't. And they're hung up there. And you say I'm gawping at them.

JANEY (*sitting in the chair* L. *of the table*). Well, you are.

(*Enter* MILLY *down* R. *She is in her dressing-gown and carries a pair of shoes wrapped up. She puts the shoes on the armchair down* R.)

MILLY. Hello.

JANEY. Hello.

JACK (*rising and moving above the easy chair*). Hello, Milly.

MILLY (*crossing below the table to the fireplace*). I've finished in the bedroom, I can do my dressing down here. (*She folds the underclothes on the horse.*)

JACK (*admiring her dressing-gown*). By gum, Milly, that's a bit of all right.

JANEY (*to* JACK). I thought you were going to pack your kitbag.

JACK (*crossing upstage to* R.). There's no hurry. Oh, I nearly forgot, I've got some blancoing to do. (*He moves to the sideboard and looks in the drawer.*)

JANEY. You're not staying in blancoing to-night, are you?

JACK. I'm on parade to-morrow, aren't I?

JANEY. Well, I think you could have done all that this afternoon. I thought you'd be takin' me jazzin'.

(MILLY *takes the underclothes upstage to the chest-of-drawers and puts them away. Then she comes downstage and moves the horse above the fire.*)

JACK. There'll be enough jazzin' for me, square-bashin' tomorrow.

JANEY. That's all very well. . . .

JACK. Aw, blimey, Janey, don't you know there's a war on?

MILLY (*moving to the chair above the fire and putting on her shoes*). I hope you don't mind me dressing down here?

JACK. No, carry on. (*He moves to the downstage* R. *corner of the table and sits on it. After a pause.*) I suppose I'd better get my kitbag fixed up.

(*He gets off the table and exits down* R. MILLY *laughs.*)

JANEY. What're you laughing at? His leave's finished, that's why he's fed up.

MILLY. Well, we'll call it that. (*She takes off her dressing-gown.*)

JANEY (*looking at* MILLY's *cami-knickers*). You didn't buy those around here.

MILLY (*putting her skirt on*). No, I didn't.

JANEY. I'd give some silk stockings for them . . . four pairs.

MILLY. Nothing doing.

JANEY. Real silk they are.

MILLY. You've got influence, haven't you?

JANEY. They didn't come from under the counter. I got them fair. Jack brought them for me, if you want to know.

MILLY. Yes, we all know that.

JANEY. You say it as though you didn't think he's every right to. We're. . . .

MILLY (*who has her skirt on by now*). Engaged. I know. Who doesn't know?

JANEY. You think you know everything, don't you?

MILLY (*moving up to the chest-of-drawers*). There's one thing I don't know, how you managed to do it?

JANEY (*smugly*). I did though, didn't I?

MILLY. There's many a slip. (*She takes her jersey from the top long drawer.*)

JANEY. What do you mean?

MILLY. What d'you think I mean?

JANEY (*rising and moving below the easy chair*). Oh! So! I thought so. My Ma said so.

MILLY. And what does your horoscope say?

JANEY (*turning to* MILLY). I knew you'd got your eye on him. (*She moves upstage towards* MILLY.) I always knew.

MILLY. He's a single man, isn't he?

JANEY. No, he isn't——

MILLY (*anticipating*). Yes, yes, we know. You're engaged. (*She puts on her jersey.*)

JANEY. Jealous, you are. That's what you are. Jealous. But you don't worry me. (*She crosses to the upstage* L. *corner of the table.*) And I don't think you look like Betty Grable with that thing on, even if you do.

MILLY. Somebody's been kidding you if you think you're a pin-up girl.

(Enter JACK *down* R. *He carries his kitbag.)*

JACK. Are you still here, Milly? *(He puts the kitbag on the armchair and moves in to* R. *of the table.)*

JANEY *(sitting on the table).* Takes her such a long time dressing up.

*(*MILLY *puts her dressing-gown in the drawer of the chest. Enter* SARAH *down* R. *with a kettle.)*

SARAH. Oh, you've shifted the bath over there, have you? Well, see you don't make a splash over everything. *(She crosses downstage to the fire. She sees* MILLY.*)* My! You won't want a torch in the blackout with that on. *(She puts the kettle on the fire and crosses downstage to* R. *and up to the sideboard.)* They'll be able to see you a mile away.

JANEY *(getting off the table and moving to the sofa).* It's specially made to attract attention.

MILLY *(coming down to the fireplace).* Seems to be succeeding, too.

JACK. Going far?

MILLY. All the way. *(She moves up to the chest-of-drawers.)*

JANEY. Bet you wish you could.

MILLY *(putting on her hat).* No harm in trying. *(She picks up a book; to* SARAH.*)* Want me to change your library book, Mrs. Hardacre?

SARAH. Try and find me summat different for a change.

MILLY. Sure. I'll find you something with love in it. Cheerio!

(She exits laughing, with the book.)

JANEY *(mocking* MILLY*).* Ha, ha, ha!

*(*SARAH *laughs.)*

JACK *(moving towards the armchair down* R.*).* Is there anything come between you two? What's to laugh at? What's to laugh at?

SARAH. There's a mirror over there, love. Have a look.

JANEY. Well, *I* don't think it's funny, and I'd like to know what we're going to do to-night, Jack Hardacre.

JACK *(crossing downstage to the fire).* I'm goin' to have a bath. *(He moves the bath round.)*

SARAH *(moving to the door down* R., *taking her apron off).* You bet you are, after all the trouble I've taken getting the bath in out of the yard and stoking the fire up. *(She hangs up her apron.)*

JANEY *(moving to the door* L. C.*).* Well, I'll wait for you at our house. P'raps you'll take me to second-house pictures.

JACK. Okay, okay. We'll land somewhere, I suppose. *(He sits in the easy chair.)*

JANEY. And don't forget I'm waiting, either.

(She goes out.)

SARAH (*taking her coat*). Now what's up, love? (*She crosses above the table towards the chest-of-drawers.*)

JACK. Nothin'—just thinkin'.

SARAH (*pausing at L. C.*). What about?

JACK. Fourteen days' leave, all but gone. Off to-morrow. (*He pauses.*) Oh, I wish war was over!

SARAH (*putting on her coat and moving to the chest-of-drawers*). Here's one wishes it never started. (*She takes her hat out of the drawer.*)

JACK. Aye, you begin to see things different when you're getting on.

SARAH (*putting her hat on top of the chest*). Getting on?

JACK. Yes—getting on!

SARAH (*crossing to L. of the table*). Getting on where?

JACK. Getting on in years, of course.

SARAH. Get away with you. You've still got cradle marks on your backside.

JACK. You're always on about my age.

SARAH. Aye, I know all about your being a grown-up soldier. Getting on, indeed! What next?

JACK. Aw, Ma! I thought you'd understand if anybody did.

SARAH (*sitting on the chair L. of the table*). Come on, lad, get it off your chest.

JACK. Aw, Ma. It's everything. I'm in a proper mess.

SARAH. Go on.

JACK. It's hard to say, like. I was only a youngster when I left here, wasn't I? Look where I've been and what I've seen these years. I'm different, I think different. I've had enough of. . . . Aw, blimey! Settled down, that's what I'd like to be. Settled down.

SARAH. Then why don't you settle down?

JACK. I mean . . . get wed.

SARAH. D'you call being wed settled down?

JACK. Give over, Ma, give over. If only I'd never given her that five quid!

SARAH. You wouldn't listen. Let yourself get half killed for five quid, and then. . . .

JACK. Half killed! I knocked him out in third round. He never touched me.

SARAH. She did, though. Five quid. Some folks never learn.

JACK. Aye, I know, Ma. I suppose I'm for it, that's all.

SARAH. If you sit there feeling sorry for yourself, you deserve to be for it.

JACK. Well, dammit all. What can a feller do? Both at me. Her and her Ma. That blasted ring——! How did I know she'd buy herself a ring? Blind old Riley, when you come to think of it, a feller's safer in the army where women are concerned.

SARAH. First you want to get out of the army and be done with soldiering and settle down, the next it's t'other way round. D'you know where you are?

JACK. You don't understand the lay of the land.

SARAH. Don't I? I've got eyes.

JACK. Oooooh! I wish I'd ne'er set eyes on Milly.

SARAH (*rising*). I've never stood in the way of anything you've wanted to do, son, and I'm not going to start now. If you don't know what you want now, you never will.

(*There is a knock at the door up* L. C. SARAH *moves upstage and opens it.*)

JACK (*rising*). Who the hell's that? (*He turns up* L. *of the easy chair.*)

(*Enter* MRS. DORBELL.)

MRS. DORBELL. It's only me. Glad I found you in, Sarah.

SARAH. Well, I'm just going out. What is it you want? . . . As though I don't know. (*She shuts the door and crosses to the sideboard.*)

MRS. DORBELL (*moving* C. *above the table and standing, cup in hand*). The usual. I've come borrowin'. (*She moves* L. C.; *to* JACK.) Eight ounces a week, and me with a sweet tooth like I've got. I was all right before my lodger died, he didn't take it.

SARAH (*moving to the table with the sugar bowl*). Oh, well, Nancy, we're rationed same as you, you know.

MRS. DORBELL. Oh, go on. And you workin' at British Restaurant. I'd go short of nowt if I worked there. (*She sits in the chair* L. *of the table.*) Eight ounces! Damn them as starts wars, I say. Can't afford a newspaper, so I'm forced to readin' t' Bible. It says, "Why do the nations so furiously rage together?"

SARAH. Ask me another. We're all supposed to have the same religion, and here they are shooting and bombing women and kids.

JACK. Ah, but——

SARAH. And I don't need any explanation from you, Jack.

JACK (*moving above the easy chair*). Look here, Ma. You can wear the trousers in this house if you like, but I'm wearing uniform. When there's muck about, somebody's got to wipe it up. It's a dirty job and nobody wants to do it, but if nobody did it what would happen to thee and the rest of the women and the kids? (*Moving to* MRS. DORBELL.) Here, give us your cup, love. Half a cup? (*He takes the cup and crosses above the table to* SARAH.)

SARAH. You'll get no half cupfuls here. And *I'll* do the dishing out, young man. (*She puts in two spoonfuls.*) That's all I can spare thee, Nancy.

(JACK *gives the cup back to* MRS. DORBELL.)

MRS. DORBELL. Eh, bless you, lass. Bless. . . .

SARAH (*turning to the sideboard and putting the sugar bowl back*). Never mind the blessings. (*She crosses towards the chest-of-drawers. To* JACK.) I've stoked the fire up for the night. And you've no need to look for the poker, because I've hid it. (*She puts on her hat.*) Leave t' fire as it is, and it'll keep in all night—and if you're staying in the rest of the evening, just sitting there gawping at the fire, you won't need the lights on, wasting money. (*She takes the menus.*) Menus, menus, menus, I'm sick of the sight, sound and smell of food! Come on, Mrs. Dorbell.

(*She exits up* L. C. MRS. DORBELL *rises and moves up to the door.* JACK *moves to the easy chair and sits on the* L. *arm.*)

MRS. DORBELL (*turning at the door*). Aren't you going out for a pint of beer to-night, Jack?

JACK. It's not beer I want, it's chloroform.

MRS. DORBELL. Get enough beer down you, and it acts pretty much the same.

JACK (*rising and putting his hand in his pocket*). Come here, Nancy. Ee! I nearly forgot.

(MRS. DORBELL *shuts the door and comes down* R. *of the easy chair.*)

There you are, it'll get you a couple of pints. (*He gives her some money.*)

MRS. DORBELL. I wasn't hinting, Jack. (*She moves* L. *to him below the easy chair. She takes the money and moves to* L. *of the table where she puts the cup down and puts the money in her purse.*)

JACK. I know you wasn't. Fourteen blooming days' leave. Thought I was goin' to enjoy 'em. Never been so bloomin' miserable in all my bloomin' life.

MRS. DORBELL. You know, Jack, I've heard 'em say as how your Ma rules you with a rod of iron. It isn't her you've to worry about. It's that other Ma of yours.

JACK. Now what're you on about? What other Ma?

MRS. DORBELL. Ma Nature. And you've no need to look at me like that. I know what I'm talking about. I ought to. I'm old enough. Nothin' to do at my time o' life but look back . . . and when I do, life seems to have been just one long day. (*She sits in the chair* L. *of the table.*) Though you don't realize the mornin' and the afternoon and the evenin's gone until it's night, and you're like me, sittin' there in that hovel, thinkin'. An' you know what, Jack——

JACK. No. What, love?

MRS. DORBELL. It's not the lads I've had in my time that I remember most. It's my childhood. I was a country girl, and I can see the cottage now. Over a brook, it was, and you crossed over a little bridge my grand-dad made out of poles he'd cut from the wood. There was a damson tree growing by the well. Trout my grand-dad used to catch out of the brook with his hands, and put them in my little apron. And he had a three-legged cat that used to bring rabbits home. In the old churchyard where my people're lying, that's where I'd like to end my days.

JACK (*crossing downstage to* R. *of the table*). Aw, chuck it, Mrs. Dorbell. Don't you think I've enough on my mind without you setting me off blubbering over thee.

MRS. DORBELL. Eh! You're a softie in the heart, Jack.

JACK (*pulling out the chair* R. *of the table and leaning on the table*). Aye, and in the bloomin' head.

MRS. DORBELL. Well, I've told you . . . and I've plenty of time to think. That's how old Ma Nature uses you. Dresses you up fit to kill in the morning, and at night even a cat wouldn't cross the road to look at you.

JACK (*crossing above the table to the fire*). Yaa! I wish they'd send me to finish off the Japs. Somewhere I can forget: a long way off.

MRS. DORBELL. Where are they sending you?

JACK. Local barracks.

MRS. DORBELL. Ah.

JACK. But I'm not getting a sleeping-out pass. I won't. Milly can have her bed back.

MRS. DORBELL. I *thought* there was a woman.

JACK. Aye. There's a woman.

(MRS. DORBELL *laughs.*)

And don't you laugh at me, you don't understand.

MRS. DORBELL. I know. Nobody understands. That's what we all think at your time of life. You wouldn't believe it, p'raps, but there was a time when I had four of 'em on a string all at the same time. If you take my tip, lad, you'd think o' me, and lose no sleep o'er the lasses.

JACK. Trouble is, Mrs. Dorbell, when she's on my mind I don't think of thee.

MRS. DORBELL. Aye, you'd be daft if you did.

JACK (*crossing below the table to* R. C.). I wish—I wish there was a cure for love.

MRS. DORBELL. There is, lad, don't you worry about that. Marriage. That'll soon cure it.

JACK (*sitting on the table*). Blimey, one I don't want and t'other I can't have.

MRS. DORBELL. Why can't you?

JACK. There's Janey, isn't there?

MRS. DORBELL. Her!

JACK. Aye, her. And her Ma. Can't call my soul my own.

MRS. DORBELL. Caught in one trap, and fretting to get out so's you can get hooked up in another.

JACK (*moving to the chair* R. *of the table and sitting*). You make it sound like a funeral.

MRS. DORBELL. That's how they all end, Jack, lad. When I look back, I ask myself, "Was it me?" and now here I am, too old to sleep—sitting in a room alone, waiting for it. (*She rises.*) Your time's very short, gone before you know you've had it. You make the most of your time, lad. (*She picks up the cup, and moves upstage.*)

JACK. That's what I want to do. But how?

MRS. DORBELL (*turning and coming in to the upstage* L. *corner of the table*). I know what I'd do if I was thee. (*She moves above the table towards* JACK.)

JACK. Oh? Aye? What?

MRS. DORBELL (*by the chair above the table*). Fate Accomply.

JACK. Eh?

MRS. DORBELL. Fate Accomply.

JACK. Fate Accomply? What's that?

MRS. DORBELL. That second 'usband of mine. Educated man, 'e was. Speak French, 'e could, though it never got him a job. Fifteen years I worked keeping him, till he died of over drinking. Ne'er had a penny in his pockets. Always wondered how he got his booze till he told me. Go from pub to pub, he used to do, he said, see a drink on the bar top, down it, then say, "I've supped it, should I ha' done?" Fate Accomply, he said.

JACK. Um. He must ha' got plenty of black eyes.

MRS. DORBELL. He got plenty of booze, too. Died of it.

JACK. Fate Accomply, eh? Ee, I wouldn't have the nerve.

MRS. DORBELL. Get a dozen doubles down you, that'd gie you the nerve.

JACK. If I did that, I wouldn't know whether I was comin' or goin'.

MRS. DORBELL. Bein' as you don't know whether you're comin' or goin' as it is, what difference does it make? (*She moves to the door up* L. C.)

JACK. Nay, I should never have come home. Biggest mistake I ever made, that was.

MRS. DORBELL. You'll find you'll be saying that all your blooming life, lad. Anyway, good night, Jack (*opening the door*), and thank you for the price of the drinks. I've given you my advice, lad, that's about all I've got to give. But you'll learn, like us all. You'll learn. Good night, lad, and bless thee. (*She opens the door wide.*)

JACK. Good night, love.

(*Exit* MRS. DORBELL.)

(*He rises and crosses above the table to the fire.*) Fate Accomply! Fate Accomply! I should never have t' nerve. Where's t' bloomin' poker gone? Oh, aye, she said she's hid it. Well, if *she's* hid it, it's hid. Blast it! (*He moves to* L. *of the table.*) Blast everything! Sufferin', that's what I am, sufferin'. Ay, I wouldn't be one of those recruits to-morrow mornin'. (*He crosses below the table to* R., *up* R. *to the sofa and picks up the book.*) She's out there; probably on her way home. . . . (*He moves to the door up* L. C., *opens it and shuts it.*) Bet Joe Truman's waiting round the corner. Joe Truman. (*He comes down to* L. *of the table.*) Joe Truman. He's free, she's free, and I'm tied up.

(*Banging the book on the table.*) Tied up, Ma, tied up. If only I hadn't
won that five pounds, Ma! If only he'd knocked me out. If—if—
if—if! Listen to me, talking to myself! Blimey, they'll be giving me
my ticket next, and putting me away. Me! *Me!* what used to
laugh at the lads when they went dizzy over the lasses. Aye—
but none of the lasses they were dizzy over were a patch on thee,
Milly. Milly . . . Millicent Southern . . . Millicent Hardacre.

> "Come, Milly, link thy arm i' mine,
> An' lilt away with me,
> An' dry that little drop of brine
> From the corner of thy e'e.
> No lordly house o' the countryside's
> So pleasant to my view——

(*He moves to the sofa and drops the book on it.*)

> As the little corner where abides
> My bonnie lass and true.
> And there's a nook." . . . (*He moves down* R.)

(MILLY *enters up* L. C. *She has a book in her hand. She takes her hat off
and puts it on the chest-of-drawers.*)

Milly, is it you?

MILLY. Why shouldn't it be? I live here, don't I? (*She comes down*
R. *of the easy chair and puts the book on the arm.*)

JACK. To think that you should come in like that just now!

MILLY. Why, how else should I come in? (*She moves to* L. *of the
table.*)

JACK. Well, you see. . . .

MILLY. I've only come in to . . . what are you looking at me like
that for? (*She crosses below the table to meet him.*)

JACK. I was just thinking of you, Milly; you know that verse my
Dad taught me? I was saying it just now when you came in. It
goes like this:

> "No lordly house o' the countryside's
> So pleasant to my view
> As the little corner where abides
> My bonnie lass and true."

But there's more to it than that.

MILLY. Is there?

JACK. Aye, much more, if only I dared say it to thee.

MILLY. Why can't you say it?

JACK. I haven't the right.

MILLY. You can say it if you want to. There's no reason why
you shouldn't finish that poem, Jack. (*She sits on the table facing
front.*)

JACK. Nay, you don't know how it goes on, Milly.

MILLY. Yes, I do.

JACK. How could you? It's a Lancashire poem.

MILLY. I know all the same.

> "And there's a nook beside yon spring,
> And if thou'll share't with me. . . ."

JACK.   "I'll buy thee the bonniest golden ring
>   That ever you did see."

Aye, lass, that's it. How did you come to learn it? I never said it to you.

MILLY. No, you haven't.

JACK. No, I shouldn't have dared.

MILLY. Well, somebody else might have been braver than you.

JACK. Aye, there's plenty braver than me. Eh! Here, wait a minute, Millicent Southern. Who's this chap that's braver than me? Tell me his name, Milly Southern. What's his name?

MILLY. Don't be silly, Jack, there's nothing to make a fuss about.

JACK. I don't know about that. I'm not at all sure about that. Was it Joe Truman? (*He crosses to* L.)

MILLY. Yes, if you want to know, it was Joe Truman.

JACK. You've been going about with him? (*He turns to* MILLY.)

MILLY. And then what?

JACK. What's been going on with you and Joe Truman?

MILLY. Is that any business of yours? (*She gets off the table and faces* JACK.)

JACK. No, it isn't, but I'm taking a hand in it all the same. I don't like it, and what's more, I won't have it. Do you hear, I won't have it!

MILLY. Yes, I can hear, I'm not deaf. (*She takes a step forward.*) Listen to me, you. I go about with whoever I please, the same as Janey Jenkins does. Only I go with chaps that want me, and if you'd like to know I've come back now to get my shoes to go dancing with Joe Truman. And you can put that in your pipe and smoke it, Mr. Jack Hardacre.

JACK (*moving in towards* MILLY). Sergeant Jack Hardacre— *Sergeant* Jack Hardacre, if you don't mind. I'm no Mister Civvy-Street-Reserved-Occupation-Foreman, chuckin' his weight about in a factory full of skirts.

MILLY. We don't wear skirts, we wear trousers.

JACK. Don't let that give you ideas. An' don't interrupt me when I'm talkin'. Joe Truman, ha! Joe Truman, braver than me, eh? Trouble with you is you don't know the difference between guts and bloomin' cheek. Well, let me tell you this, if Joe Truman wants a basinful o' trouble, he's going the right way about getting it.

MILLY. Don't be a fool, Jack. What's the use of talking that way? Besides, those verses aren't your property.

JACK. You're not his property either.

MILLY. I'm nobody's property.

JACK. Yes you are. You're mine.

MILLY. Oh, since when, pray?

JACK. Ever since that first day I stood there like what Ma called a moonstruck calf, gawping at you. That's true, isn't it, Milly love? Say it's true, Milly love! (*He takes her hand.*)

(*Enter* JANEY *up* L. C. JACK *and* MILLY *turn upstage.*)

JANEY (*coming down* L. C.). Oh!

JACK. What d'you mean, "Oh"?

JANEY. So this is why I've been kept waiting for you, Jack Hardacre!

JACK. Blimey! Didn't I tell you I was going to have a bath? (*He crosses below the table to* R. *and up to the chair* R. *of it.*)

JANEY. Yes, you did.

JACK. Well, I haven't had it yet, see? See? See? (*He sits* R. *of the table.*)

JANEY. I can see you haven't. An' it's not the only thing I can see.

MILLY. What else can you see?

JANEY. I can see both of you alone in this house, and him with his boots off and half undressed.

JACK. JANEY!!

JANEY. An' her bed nice and handy.

JACK. That'll be enough from you, Janey.

JANEY. All worked out nice and proper, hasn't it?

MILLY. You little cat, what d'you mean?

JANEY. Cat, am I? Ho! And what sort of an animal do you think you are?

MILLY (*crossing to* JANEY). One that won't take any backchat from you.

JANEY. Yes and I won't take any cheek from you.

MILLY. You be quiet!

(*Enter* JOE TRUMAN *up* L. C.)

JOE. Are you ready, Milly? (*He shuts the door and crosses down* L.) I thought I heard voices, so I came in.

JACK. Come in, Joe. Come in, leave the door open, let 'em all come in. We only live here.

JOE. Are you ready, Milly?

JANEY. She's ready, Joe Truman, ready for anybody.

MILLY. I've had enough of this—come on, Joe. (*She crosses to the chair down* R. *for her shoes and up* R. *to the sofa for her coat.*)

JANEY (*moving in to* L. *of the table and speaking across it*). About time too, then perhaps Jack can have his bath in peace. Come on Jack. (*She crosses to* R. *of him.*) I'll give you a hand with your shirt and a back scrub. (*Behind him.*) I've not forgotten how to do it.

JOE (*going up* L. C. *to the door*). Well, come on, Milly, if you're ready.

MILLY. Wait!

JOE ⎱ (*together*). ⎰ Here, but what's all this about?
JANEY ⎰   ⎱ (*Moving above the table.*) You be off, Joe Truman, and her with you, you're neither of you wanted.

MILLY. But you're not going to . . . Jack. . . .

JOE ⎱ (*together*). ⎰ If you ask me, this is a bit of. . . .
JANEY ⎰   ⎱ It's all ready, Jack.

JACK (*rising and moving above the table to* C.). Here, here, all of you——

MILLY. Oh, go away, Joe, go away.

JOE ⎱ (*together*). ⎰ But, Milly, what's all this about?
JANEY ⎰   ⎱ Come on, outside the pair of you.

JACK. 'Ere, 'ere, all of you, just a minute, just a minute! Open front door and fetch all street in! Bring back brass band. Sit yourselves down. I'm only going to get undressed and have a bath.

(*All speak at once.*)

Come on, sit yourselves down and make yourselves comfortable!

(*All speak at once.*)

Blimey, for sheer peace and quiet give me the bloody barrage at El Alamein! (*He begins to take off his shirt.*)

CURTAIN

ACT III

Scene: *The "Flying Shuttle". Evening. A suitable time later.*

The table at c. has been moved upstage in front of the bench.

When the curtain *rises* Mrs. Dorbell *is sitting* c. *on the bench with a glass of bitter.* Joe Truman *is on the upstage stool at the counter with an empty glass.*

Joe. Another whisky, Harry.

Lancaster. That will be one and six. (*He puts a glass of whisky on the counter.*)

Joe. I've told you before, I've put me money on the bar. Take it from there.

Mrs. Dorbell. Doing yourself well, aren't you, Joe? Tryin' to drown your sorrows?

Joe. No, tryin' to mind my own business.

Mrs. Dorbell. You'll find it difficult in these parts.

Joe. Aye. I can see that.

Mrs. Dorbell. You look as though you've got all the troubles of the world on your shoulders.

Joe. I've enough to keep me busy.

Mrs. Dorbell. Well, you're going the right way to drown 'em. If you'd take my tip, you'd stick to bitter. (*She holds her glass up ostentatiously to see how much remains in it. Then she makes a long-winded attempt to find her purse.*) Purse gone again.

Joe. Give her one, Harry. Give her one.

Mrs. Dorbell. Thank you, Joe. I wasn't hinting. Just going to order it. (*She rises and takes her glass to the counter.*) Purse keeps falling down the hole in my placket.

(Lancaster *puts a glass of Guinness on the counter.*)

Joe. I know.

Mrs. Dorbell. You've no need to say it as though you don't believe me. (*She drinks.*)

Joe. Sup up and have less to say.

Mrs. Dorbell. Things're pretty quiet in here to-night, Harry.

Lancaster. It's a change.

Mrs. Dorbell. Eh, I did enjoy that do we had in the street for Jack Hardacre.

Lancaster. Pie was gradely. Rare hand at cooking is Sarah Hardacre.

MRS. DORBELL. He's coming home to-night, Jack is.

LANCASTER. Is he?

JOE. When's he getting wed?

MRS. DORBELL. Who to?

JOE. Who to? Why, Janey Jenkins, o' course. They're engaged, aren't they?

MRS. DORBELL. From what I've seen o' the carryin' on around here during the war, *marriage* means nothin', never mind engagements. Not as I blame anybody for what they want to do.

JOE. Give us another, Harry. (*He pushes his empty glass forward.*)

MRS. DORBELL. *She's* started.

JOE. Who?

MRS. DORBELL. Her that lives along o' Sarah Hardacre. Milly.

JOE. Started what?

MRS. DORBELL. Drinkin'.

JOE. What!

MRS. DORBELL. Drinkin' Guinness.

JOE (*half to himself*). Guinness! Milly drinkin'. An' never used to touch it at all.

MRS. DORBELL. If she feels as if she wants it. . . . (*She laughs.*)

LANCASTER. That'll be quite enough, Nancy. That'll be quite enough.

MRS. DORBELL. What's up with thee?

LANCASTER. No scandalizing. Not in my pub.

MRS. DORBELL. Scandalizing? Me, scandalizing? I like that!

LANCASTER. Well, I don't.

JOE. What do you mean? (*He lights a cigarette.*)

MRS. DORBELL. I've said nothing but what's plain as the nose on your face for everybody to see.

LANCASTER. And I've told thee. No scandalizing, or sup up and outside.

MRS. DORBELL. That's right. Every time I come in I'm chucked out. You've never been the same since we had that tater pie do in the street.

LANCASTER. Never mind that.

MRS. DORBELL. *You* haven't got your eyes on young Milly by any chance, have you?

LANCASTER. It'd be no business of yours if I had. I'm single . . . *and* I've got brass.

JOE. You don't mean to say that you. . . .

LANCASTER. I'm saying nowt, Joe.

JOE. That's all very well. . . .

LANCASTER. And I'll serve thee no more, Mrs. Dorbell. You can find another pub. See what you've started?

MRS. DORBELL. You'll have to serve me if I order a drink. That's the law of the land.

LANCASTER. It is not the law of the land.

MRS. DORBELL. Oho, yes it is.

LANCASTER. Oho, no it isn't.

JOE. Well, 'Arry, I don't like either the sound or the smell of it.

LANCASTER. That'll do, Joe. Even if you're one of my *best* customers.

MRS. DORBELL. Never you mind, Joe. The war won't last for ever. He'll be glad of our custom then. And so will a few more o' them wi' shops.

LANCASTER. I've told thee before, Mrs. Dorbell. Sup up and outside.

MRS. DORBELL. In my own time. In my own time. I'm chokin' myself for nobody.

A VOICE (*in the Public Bar*). Give us a bitter, Harry.

ANOTHER VOICE. Mild will do for me.

(LANCASTER *moves upstage to serve the order.*)

MRS. DORBELL. Ha! It'd be a fine how-do-you-do wouldn't it?

JOE. What would?

MRS. DORBELL. If Milly went off with him.

JOE. Gaa! ! Go on.

MRS. DORBELL (*laughing*). You heard what he said. About havin' the brass.

JOE. Gaa! ! He's old enough to be her father!

MRS. DORBELL (*laughing*). Ha!

JOE (*sourly*). Ha! Ha!

MRS. DORBELL. Old enough to be her father!

JOE. So he is.

MRS. DORBELL. What she'd lose on the swings she'd gain on the roundabouts. (*She laughs.*)

JOE. You've got it all worked out, haven't you?

(LANCASTER *enters through the door* C.)

MRS. DORBELL (*sniffing*). Well, Joe. All I've got to say is, you mark my words.

LANCASTER. I'm markin' 'em. (*He moves to* L. C.)

MRS. DORBELL. Go on then, mark 'em. (*She sips her Guinness.*)

LANCASTER. I shan't tell you again. Outside you'll go, and the Guinness with you.

MRS. DORBELL (*thoroughly irritated*). Aw! (*She drains the glass, and crosses down* R.) Go to hell!

LANCASTER. Mind your language.

MRS. DORBELL. Worse than an old woman, you are. Thank God I'm not married to thee!

(*She exits down* R.)

JOE. Who wants to get married anyway?

LANCASTER. A fellow can do many a worse thing.

JOE. Then you *are* thinking about it.

LANCASTER. I'm sayin' nowt. (*He crosses to the counter.*)

JOE. Is it Milly?

LANCASTER. You've got a tongue. (*As he turns and crosses to the door* C.) Why don't you ask her?

JOE. Don't fret yourself. Sick I am o' being kept dangling.

A VOICE (*from the Public Bar*). Pint o' mild, Rosie.

(*Exit* LANCASTER C.)

JOE. Fed up, that's what I am. Fed up. Chucked myself at her. That's what I did. Then she treats me as though I'm a doormat. Serves me right. I should ha' known better. Aw! (*He flings his cigarette away.*)

(LANCASTER *comes downstage behind the counter.*)

LANCASTER. Somebody come in, Joe?

JOE. I saw nobody.

LANCASTER. Could ha' sworn I heard you talking to somebody.

JOE. You don't want to believe all you hear.

LANCASTER. All right, keep your hair on——

(*Enter* MILLY *down* R.)

JOE. Hello, Milly.

LANCASTER. 'Evening, miss.

MILLY (*crossing to the counter*). Good evening. The usual, please.

(LANCASTER *puts a bottle of Guinness on the counter.* MILLY *pays and puts the bottle in her bag.*)

Thank you. Good night. (*She crosses towards* R.)

JOE (*getting off the stool and crossing towards* R.). What's up, Milly?

MILLY (*turning at* R.). With what?

(LANCASTER *moves upstage.*)

JOE. With me. You never even said "good evening".

MILLY. Oh, I'm sorry, Joe. Good evening.

JOE. Won't you have a drink, lass?

MILLY. I've got one, thanks.

JOE. I don't know what's come over you, Milly. You make me feel I've done summat . . . or said summat . . . to offend you.

MILLY. Don't be silly, Joe. Of course you haven't.

JOE. Ay! I'm glad of that, Milly. But I wish you'd come out with me, once in a while.

MILLY. I'm sorry. I've got other things to do.

JOE. You've said that before. You've never been the same since Jack Hardacre came home. There was a time when I thought me and thee were. . . .

MILLY. What?

JOE. You know . . . hit it off.

MILLY. I only went out with you twice.

JOE. Aye . . . but. . . . Oh, in these parts . . . but it may be different in London. (*He turns away from* MILLY.)

MILLY. What on earth are you trying to say?

JOE. It's very embarrassin'.

MILLY. I've heard *that* one before.

JOE. Eh?

MILLY. Skip it.

JOE (*jealously*). That sounded like that there American officer.

MILLY. So what?

JOE. You see! That's another of the things he used to say.

MILLY. What is?

JOE. So what.

MILLY. Well? So what? (*She crosses in front of* JOE *to* R. *of the table*.)

JOE (*following her*). Nay, lass, nay. Don't thee go, don't thee go.

MILLY. Don't you start on me with that dialect.

JOE (*puzzled*). Why, love, what's. . . ?

MILLY. All these "thees" and "thous" and "Don't thee go". It does *summat* to me. Now, there.

JOE. Eh, you're a funny girl.

MILLY. Am I?

JOE. Ay, lass. Eh! You're so champion I can't. . . . What's the use of talking?

(MILLY *turns and moves to cross* JOE *towards the door*.)

(*Pleading*.) Nay, Milly, love. Won't you stay? Just a few minutes longer. I tell thee, lass, I'm bein' driven nuts.

MILLY. That's American, Joe. I thought you couldn't stand it.

JOE (*crossing to the counter*). Well, daft, then. Daft. That's what I'm being driven. Morning, noon and night you're on my mind.

MILLY (*crossing towards* JOE). Now Joe, this has got to stop.

JOE (*with his back to her, leaning on the counter*). What's the use o' saying that? Can't you see, I'm blind, bow-legged and barmy about thee.

(MILLY *laughs*.)

That's it. Laugh at me. Finish me off, proper. Go on. Laugh.

MILLY. Oh, Joe, I wasn't laughing at you. It's the things you say.

JOE. There was me thinking you'd at least have a spark of understanding. Why didn't you stop me from telling you all I've just been carrying on about.

MILLY. It's no use, Joe. And that must be the end of it.

JOE (*turning to her*). But. . . ? Why? What's wrong wi' me?

MILLY. Nothing.

JOE. Ay, lass, I wish you meant it.

MILLY. Of course I do.

JOE. You mean you really like me?

MILLY. I said I thought you were nice. But there's nothing more than that.

JOE. Is there anybody else?

MILLY. Now, Joe, that's got nothing to do with it.

JOE. It's Jack Hardacre, isn't it?

MILLY. I'm going. (*She turns and crosses to* R.)

JOE (*following her*). Milly——

MILLY (*stopping at the door down* R.). What is it?

JOE. Let's walk with thee.

MILLY. No.

JOE. Milly. Milly. Please.

MILLY. No.

JOE. I'm coming with you.

MILLY. You're forgetting yourself, Joe Truman. If you dare to set one foot out of the door after me, I'll never speak to you again.

JOE. I'm. . . .

MILLY. You ought to be ashamed of yourself—you're drunk, Joe Truman.

(*She exits.*)

JOE. Drunk. Said I was drunk, she did. Drunk, am I? Drunk, eh? (*He crosses to the front of the table* C. *and sits on it.*)

(LANCASTER *comes downstage behind the counter.*)

LANCASTER. What's up wi' thee? Sitting there chunnering to yourself?

JOE. Thee shut thy trap.

LANCASTER. Art talking to me?

JOE (*getting off the table and crossing to the counter upstage*). I'm not chewin' a brick. And thee gie me a double.

LANCASTER. I'll gie thee a double backhander if you talk to me like that.

(*Enter down* R. MRS. JENKINS, MRS. DORBELL, TED MUNTER *and* CHARLIE FOX.)

MRS. JENKINS (*crossing to the* R. *end of the bench*). I'm glad to have a set down, anyway. (*She sits.*)

LANCASTER. Hey! Mrs. Dorbell—outside.

MRS. DORBELL (*crossing up* L.). Save your breath, save your breath, if you're thinkin' of hordering me hout. I've been invited. (*To* MUNTER.) And that's a fact, isn't it, Ted? (*She sits on the bench,* L. *end.*)

MUNTER (*moving up* C.). That's right. Set 'em up, Harry, drinks all round. (*He stands by the door* C.)

JOE. I can buy my own.

MUNTER. Please yourself, it's money in my pocket.

MRS. JENKINS. Mine's a bitter, Mr. Lancaster. That'll do for me.

MRS. DORBELL. Mine's a Guinness, please, Ted.

CHARLIE (*crossing to the counter below* JOE). It won't do for me. I'll have a double. You'd better give Ted a couple, he's been shouting the odds at the dogs all afternoon.

LANCASTER. He's not the only one been shouting the odds.

JOE. Don't start on me, Harry Lancaster, I've had enough for to-night.

LANCASTER. That's easy to see. You'll get no more to-night; not in here you won't.

MUNTER (*crossing the counter between* CHARLIE *and* JOE). What's going on in here?

LANCASTER⎫ (*together*). ⎧Nowt I can't manage.
JOE　　　　⎭　　　　　⎩Thee keep out of it.

MRS. DORBELL. What's up with everybody to-night? I'm beginning to think there's no place like home.

MUNTER (*slapping* JOE *on the back*). What's up wi' thee, Joe lad?

JOE. Nowt.

MUNTER. Pay for them, Charlie.

LANCASTER. That'll be seven and six. (*He puts a bitter, a Guinness and two doubles on the counter.*)

(CHARLIE *passes the bitter and Guinness to* MRS. JENKINS *and* MRS. DORBELL.)

MUNTER (*imperiously*). Have one yourself, Harry.

LANCASTER. That'll be nine shillings.

(CHARLIE *moves to the downstage end of the counter and pays.*)

MUNTER (*turning to* L. C. *and raising his glass*). Here's hoping I ne'er have a worse afternoon at the dogs.

CHARLIE. The money that's knocking about now! (*He sits on the downstage stool.*)

MRS. DORBELL. Wish a chunk'd find its way to my pocket.

MUNTER (*turning to* JOE). What is matter wi' thee, Joe? You're acting like a bear wi' a sore head.

MRS. JENKINS. I've a good idea. Here's to you, Ted. Good health!

MUNTER. Good health, girls! (*He turns to the counter.*)

MRS. DORBELL. Thought we should have had a wedding in the street before now, now that Jack Hardacre's back.

MRS. JENKINS. What d'you mean, Mrs. Dorbell?

MRS. DORBELL. Jack and your Janey, o' course. (*She sips her drink.*) No signs yet, I notice.

LANCASTER (*warningly*). H'm. . . .

MRS. JENKINS. Go on, Mrs. Dorbell. Go on, I'm listening. Go on.

MRS. DORBELL. Not B. likely. This is a free country, this is, and I've been ordered out of here to-night once already for speaking my mind.

Mrs. Jenkins. They'll get married when it suits 'em.

Lancaster. Now, Mrs. Jenkins!

Mrs. Dorbell. Told you so.

Mrs. Jenkins. We was only talking about Janey and Jack Hardacre. Silk stockings he brought her home. Bet she's the only girl round here got 'em. An' lipstick and nail varnish and face colouring. Enough to open a shop he brought.

Mrs. Dorbell. H'm. Some of 'em need it.

Mrs. Jenkins. What d'you mean by that, Mrs. Dorbell?

Munter (*moving to* c. *of the bench; saving the situation*). Used to be sweet on a lass myself when I was young. Pretty as a picture. Kep' awake all night thinkin' about her. Ah! but she wouldn't look at me. Married a piano player what couldn't earn salt to his porridge. Saw her a couple o' weeks ago. Couldn't believe my eyes. Rolling along like a barrel she was. (*He crosses to the counter.*)

Charlie. Makes you think, Ted lad. It makes you think. (*He chuckles.*)

Mrs. Dorbell. I never see thee out with a lass, Charlie.

Charlie. I go where I'm not known. Always leave the back door open, that's my motto.

Munter. Wise guy. Sleeps with his socks on.

Lancaster. You be careful. A lot of the lads who've been abroad're back. And they're not in the mood, Charlie. They're not in the mood.

Charlie. Ay, you've no need to worry about me. I know when to get me skates on.

Munter. I know how they feel. Two years in Flanders and eighteen months in Italy, that's what I had, in the last war.

Charlie (*getting off the stool*). Labour Corps, that was me—— (*He crosses to the bench and sits at* Mrs. Dorbell's r.) Walk, that's what we had to do in the last shindy. None of your jeeps and trucks. Four years of it and lost all I earned at Crown and Anchor.

Mrs. Dorbell. That'll larn you.

Joe. Well, I'm fed up with the blooming war.

Munter (*pushing his glass forward*). Nark it. Fill 'em up, Harry, same again. (*He turns to* l. c.) Reckon this country's going to be worth livin' in after the war. (*He offers cigarettes to* Joe, Charlie *and* Lancaster.) What with the dole, Beveridge Report, Public Assistance and Old Age Pensions at two quid a week. I wouldn't mind bein' a workin' man again myself. (*He turns to the counter.*)

(Lancaster *puts a bitter, a Guinness and two doubles on the counter.*)

Charlie (*rising and crossing to the counter*). You can have it, Ted. Work saw the last of me soon as I got my civvy suit on after the last war. (*He takes the bitter, Guinness and a double to the table* c.) Me in the trenches while other blokes stopped at home makin' fortunes on munitions.

JOE. That one for me?

CHARLIE. I'm talking about the last war.

MUNTER. You've no need to be quarrelsome, Joe—Look at us. All happy and jolly, just what I like to see.

A VOICE (*in the Public Bar*). It's true what I tell you.

BARMAID (*in the Public Bar*). Now, Mr. Brierley, behave yourself.

(*General laughter from the Public Bar.*)

MUNTER. And hark at them in there. (*He crosses to the table* C. *with his drink.*) Who've you got next door, Harry? (*He puts his drink on the table.*)

LANCASTER. Quite a tidy lot, not doing so bad these days.

MUNTER (*crossing to the door* C.). I've arranged a little scrap over at Oldham. Is Jack Hardacre there? I want to tell him about it, and get it all fixed up.

(*He exits into the Public Bar.* CHARLIE *leaves his drink on the table* C. *and follows* MUNTER.)

A VOICE (*in the Public Bar*). Listen to Bob here. . . .

MRS. JENKINS (*calling after* MUNTER). No, Jack hasn't come in yet, Mr. Munter. . . . Oh, he's gone. Yes, I don't mind saying I'm waiting for Jack Hardacre. Our Janey's not at all satisfied with the ways he's been going on. Quite time they was married and settled down, I say.

MRS. DORBELL. Have you told 'im so?

MRS. JENKINS. I've written to 'im. That's why he's coming.

LANCASTER. Aw, Mrs. Jenkins, there's a war on, you know. He'll settle down when it's over.

MRS. DORBELL. If a lass can't catch a 'usband when there's a war on, she'll never get one at all.

MRS. JENKINS. What do you mean, "catch a 'usband"? And don't talk to me about the war. I'm sick of it.

MRS. DORBELL. Three wars there's been in my time, and I'm still as hard up as I ever was, and we won 'em all.

JOE (*moving to the downstage end of the counter*). Well, I'm fed up with it too. Damned glad to get into a uniform if they'd let me.

MRS. DORBELL. You'd be a damned sight gladder to get out of it.

JOE. Everybody looking at you as though you was dodging the column. Everybody thinkin' you're making a fortune. Half of it stopped for income tax. Two and fourpence for a shillin' packet of fags. Beer like water, and look at the price of it.

MRS. JENKINS. That's what I say. (*She looks at* MRS. DORBELL.) When you've got to pay for your own.

LANCASTER. Well, it doesn't go into my pocket.

(JOE *attempts to sit on the downstage stool. He misjudges the distance, slips, and almost falls over the stool.*)

(*To* JOE.) Steady on, lad.

JOE. I suppose you all think I'm drunk. Well, I'll drink anyone here under the table.

LANCASTER. Not in here you won't.

(*Enter* JACK *down* R.)

JACK (*at the door*). Hullo, Harry!

LANCASTER. Hullo there, Jack.

JACK. Hullo, Nancy!

MRS. JENKINS. Hullo, Jackie.

JACK. Good evening, Mrs. Jenkins.

LANCASTER. You been home, Jack?

JACK. Not yet.

MRS. JENKINS. Oh, you've come, then, have you?

(LANCASTER *moves upstage.*)

JACK. Aye. By special request, it seems.

MRS. JENKINS. You got my note then, Jackie?

JACK (*crossing to the counter above* JOE). I did. And I can do without the "Jackie", too—I don't like it, see?

MRS. JENKINS. Oh, you don't, don't you? Well, there's things I don't like either, and our Janey's feeling the same way, too. Waiting she is, waiting over at our house.

JACK. Why didn't she come over here with you? You knew I'd be coming. Seeing as you asked me. You make it sound as though I'm running away.

MRS. JENKINS. Nay, nay, lad. Run away? You? And our Janey engaged. It's the ring that binds, you know.

JACK. It is, is it?

(CHARLIE *enters* C.)

CHARLIE (*entering*). Hullo, Jack. (*He calls to* MUNTER *in the Public Bar.*) Here's Jack, Ted. (*He crosses to the counter above* JACK.)

(MUNTER *enters* C.)

MUNTER (*entering and crossing to* R. *of* JACK). I see you are, lad, and what I want to know is, when are you going back?

JACK. Say that again.

MUNTER. When're you going back?

JACK (*glaring and jerking his thumb*). Outside!

MUNTER. What's up? (*He backs downstage towards* L.)

JACK. You. Outside.

MUNTER. What've I done?

(MRS. DORBELL *drinks one of the doubles on the table* C.)

JACK. It isn't what you've done, it's what you've said.

MUNTER. What I said?

JACK. Yes, what you said. You said, "Hullo, Jack! Home agen,

when're you goin' back?" Come on. Outside! (*He moves towards*
MUNTER.)

MUNTER. Nay, nay, I'm old enough to be thy father.

JACK. If you was old enough to be my great-great-great-great-
grandfather, it wouldn't make any difference. (*He jerks his thumb
again.*) Come on. Get out.

MRS. JENKINS. It's all friendly-like, Jack.

CHARLIE. Ay, Jack, you've no need. . . .

JACK. Be quiet——

MRS. JENKINS. No need at all. . . .

JACK. ——both of you!

MRS. JENKINS. Well, Jack Hardacre. Talking to me like that,
and I don't know what's come over you. It's just what our Janey
says.

JOE. That's right, that's right, everybody keep your traps shut.
We're only civvies.

JACK. Oho. You, too, eh?

(MUNTER *backs farther away to* R. *of the table* C.)

JOE. Aye. Me, too.

(MRS. DORBELL *drinks the other double on the table* C.)

JACK. Okay. The three of you. Come on. I'll take the lot on.

(LANCASTER *enters* C.)

LANCASTER. Here, here, what's this?

JACK. You anything to say? (*He crosses to* LANCASTER.)

(MUNTER *moves farther* R.)

LANCASTER. Aye. I have. If you're not out of this place right
away, I'll call the cops. (*To the others.*) You all stay where you are.
(*To* JACK.) And remember this, you. You're not the only one that
knows what the army's like. We had our packet twenty years ago.

CHARLIE. Aye. Aye. That's a fact.

MUNTER. Aye. Four years in France. No leave and up to the
eyes in. . . .

LANCASTER (*to* MUNTER). Language! Language!

MUNTER. Up to the eyes in it, anyway. And only a bob a day.
So there's nowt you can tell us, Jack Hardacre, what we don't
know already.

CHARLIE. Come on, Jack lad—have another drink. Harry, give
him one.

LANCASTER. Well, I'll serve his drinks so long as it's understood
that there's no more disturbance in this pub.

MUNTER. That's right, Harry lad, fill 'em up! Drinks all round
again.

JACK. I'm not drinking any more at the moment, Ted Munter.

MRS. JENKINS. No, you'd be better tempered if you did.

MUNTER. Aye, you would.

JACK (*to* MUNTER). Come on outside and get what's coming to you.

MRS. JENKINS. Nay, JACK lad. He didn't mean nowt.

(*Exit* LANCASTER C.)

CHARLIE (*to* JACK). What's it matter, anyway?

MUNTER. We'll drink to your health coupled with the name of Miss Janey Jenkins.

JACK. You can say that outside, too. Go on, get out!

MUNTER. Come on, Charlie.

(*Exit* MUNTER *down* R.)

JACK (*to* CHARLIE). And you can listen to him saying it.

(CHARLIE *crosses and exits down* R.)

Wait for me out there, I'll be with you directly. Don't run away. (*He turns at* R. C.) Now Joe Truman, your turn next. Come on.

(LANCASTER *comes downstage behind the counter.*)

LANCASTER. Where's Ted Munter and Charlie Fox?

MRS. DORBELL. Gone to powder their noses.

LANCASTER. Oh!

MRS. JENKINS (*rising and crossing to the door down* R.). I'll just slip across and tell our Janey you're here. Gettin' ready, she was, when I came out. All that face stuff you brought her.

(*She exits down* R. JACK *makes a gesture of relief.*)

LANCASTER. Where's them drinks Ted Munter and Charlie Fox left? Two doubles.

MRS. DORBELL (*rising and crossing* R. C.; *to* JACK). I've supped them. Should I have done?

JACK. That's fate accomply, that is.

LANCASTER. What does that mean?

JACK. Remind me to tell you, some time. And you can put the drinks down to me.

MRS. DORBELL. Thank you, Jack. Suppose you're entered for the matrimonial stakes now, eh?

JACK. Well, there's no harm in supposin'.

MRS. DORBELL. It'd do my heart good to see a well set-up lad like thee married.

JACK. Aye—shouldn't wonder. There was four unmarried fellows in here just now. Somebody's got to take on the job. (*He crosses to the counter, upstage end.*)

MRS. DORBELL. Birth rate's going down.

JACK. That's what you think. (*He pays for the two doubles and sits on the upstage stool.*)

MRS. DORBELL (*at the door* C.). I'll bet every feller'll be made to have a couple of wives soon.

(She exits into the Public Bar.)

JOE. Three times I've tried to join the blinking army, and they've blooming well turned me down. Fed up, I am, with the war and uniforms. Anythin' in a uniform. It'll be Eyetie and Jerry prisoners of war next. What chance has a civvy got with a woman? To hell wi' war and uniforms, I say, and give us all a fair do from scratch.

JACK *(kindly)*. What's on thy mind, Joe lad? *(He looks at* LANCASTER.*)* What's got hold of him?

LANCASTER. I've already told him . . . he's had too much to. . . .

JOE. That I haven't. Sober as a judge, I am. Aye, and I can prove it. *(He crosses to* R. C., *takes off his coat, throws it down at* L. C., *and turns to* JACK.*)* Chalk a line on t' bloody floor, and. . . .

LANCASTER. Shan't tell thee again about language.

JOE. Drunk, am I?

LANCASTER. Aye, stinkin' drunk.

JOE. Am I drunk, Jack? Look at me.

JACK. Well, there's summat wrong wi' thee, Joe.

A VOICE *(from the Public Bar)*. Ask 'em to shout louder in there. We can't hear.

LANCASTER. You're not supposed to, it's private.

*(*LANCASTER *moves upstage.* JOE *sits on the bench,* R. *end.)*

JACK. You'll have a fat head in the mornin', Joe.

JOE. I've got one now. I've always had one. Fat head, that's me.

JACK. Well, you ought to know. You've been carrying it around long enough.

JOE. I want to know where I stand.

JACK. You're in t' "Flying Shuttle", an' your jacket's on t' floor. Put it on, and go home and rest.

JOE. Rest? How can I rest wi' what I've got on my mind?

JACK. Well, what *is* on your mind, Joe? Have you got some wench into trouble?

JOE. Nay. I'm the one that's in trouble.

JACK. I've never heard o' that happenin' before. *(He gets off the stool and turns to the counter.)*

JOE. Never been the same to me, she hasn't, since you came home.

JACK. Are you talking about Milly?

JOE. Aye, I am.

JACK. I could have told you you were wasting your time. You're too late, Joe.

JOE. Supposin' I don't think so?

JACK *(kindly)*. You've no need to get shirty, Joe. I can well understand your feelings. I've had a basinful myself.

JOE. I want none o' thy sympathy, Jack Hardacre. What about her you're engaged to already? Who dost think thou art— Solomon?

JACK (*sitting on the stool*). Aye, what about her? That's it. What about her? I wish I knew. (*He drinks.*) Take my advice, lad, and forget all about it.

JOE. Don't thee talk so daft. It isn't as easy as that. It isn't like goin' round to the dentist and having a tooth out. It's here. (*He puts his hand to his heart, then puts his head in his hands and leans on the table.*)

JACK (*rising*). Tell me something I don't know. (*He moves to the bench and sits* L. *of* JOE.) But cryin' won't help thee.

JOE. Who's cryin'?

JACK. Thou art. Near as dammit.

JOE (*sobbing*). I won't give her up. . . .

JACK (*putting an arm on* JOE's *shoulder*). Settle your mind to it, Joe, settle your mind to it, Joe. We've got name for the baby.

(MRS. DORBELL *looks in round the door* C. *and* LANCASTER *from above the partition behind the bar.*)

JOE (*to* JACK). Here, what's that you're saying?

JACK. John Bernard Montgomery Hardacre, if it's a lad, an' Millicent Elizabeth if it's a lass. After the General and the Princess, tha knows.

JOE. You mean Milly is. . . .

JACK. Aye, there's the truth for you, Joe. There's the truth for you.

LANCASTER. Does your Ma know of this?

JACK (*rising*). Ructions, that's what there's going to be. Ructions.

MRS. DORBELL. Aye, there will be ructions—and what about our Janey? Does she and her Ma know?

JACK (*going to the counter*). There's only one consolation where Janey is concerned. Fate accomply. Give us another drink.

MRS. DORBELL. Oh, I see. Black eyes, you said. There'll be scratched faces this time. So long, Jack.

(*She exits down* R. JOE *sobs.*)

JACK. Nay, Joe. That won't do thee any good. You're feeling sorry for yourself. Stop your bellyaching. Think what I've got on my plate with Janey. Be a man, man!

JOE. A man, eh? Well, I'll tell you what. I wouldn't mind. No, I wouldn't.

JACK. What's your blather now?

JOE. I shouldn't mind taking her on all the same.

JACK. Who? Janey?

JOE. Janey my foot! Milly, I mean, baby and all. Her father's nowt to me and will be nowt to her soon.

JACK. Oh, I'm nowt, am I? Thee wait and see whether I come through the war or not before you start makin' a widder out of her.

JOE. Well, I wouldn't mind havin' a do at makin' a widder of her right now. (*He rises and crosses down* R.) I will have a do, even if you murder me.

JACK. I warn you, I *will* murder you.

JOE. D'you hear? Even if you murder me.

(*Enter* SARAH, MILLY, JANEY, MRS. JENKINS *and* MRS. DORBELL, *down* R. JOE *rushes at* JACK, *misses and falls on the counter.*)

MRS. DORBELL		Fightin'! Fightin'! There you are! What did I tell you? (*She stands* R. *of the door* C.)
JANEY	(*together*).	Stop 'em! Oh, stop 'em, Ma!
SARAH		(*Crossing to* L. C.) What's all this? What's all this?
MRS. JENKINS		It's come to a head at last, has it?

(MILLY, JANEY *and* MRS. JENKINS *remain in a group down* R.)

JACK (*picking up* JOE's *coat and throwing it on* JOE). Put thy jacket on.

JOE. I won't put my coat on. (*He flings the coat on the floor and rushes* JACK *again.*)

(JACK *catches him by the arm and twists him round over the counter.*)

SARAH. You keep out o' this, Ma Jenkins. It's nowt to do with you.

MRS. JENKINS. Nowt to do with me, eh? Hear that, our Janey? I'll have you know that our Janey. . . .

SARAH. Our Janey wants to go home and have a good scrub to take some of that red raddle off her face and finger-ends.

JANEY. Oh, Ma! She's always had it in for me.

SARAH. Shut up.

LANCASTER. That'll be enough of that. Mrs. Hardacre . . . this is still my pub, you know.

SARAH. And you shut up, too.

LANCASTER. Thank God it's closing time. Time, gentlemen, please!

(*He moves upstage into the Public Bar.*)

SARAH. What's your coat doin' on t' floor, Joe Truman? Makin' a doormat out of it?

JOE (*crossing* R. *and picking up his coat*). Doormat! Aye! That's me, a bloomin' doormat. And all the chances I had with the others, and ne'er took one of them.

SARAH. What've you bin doing to the lad, our Jack?

JACK (*loudly*). I never touched him.

SARAH. Well, what's it all about?

MILLY (*crossing to* L. *of the table; to* JACK). Now, Jack Hardacre, this is where you dig your toes in. No Munich stuff and running away.

JACK. Running away? Who's running away?

JANEY (*moving to* R. *of the table and confronting* MILLY *across it*). Who are you ordering about, Milly Southern. Whose young man do you think he is?

MILLY. I'll drop you a line and let you know.

MRS. JENKINS. Of all the brazen impudence—I never heard. . . .

(LANCASTER *enters* C.)

SARAH (*crossing down* L.). Listen! Listen! Listen! Will you stop all this riddle-me-reeing and let's know what all this is about?

MRS. DORBELL. I'll tell you. That lass is having a child. And if you can't tell when a lass that's living with you is in the family way, Sarah, then you've been a widder too long.

LANCASTER (*taking* MRS. DORBELL *by the scruff of the neck*). Aye, and *you've* been in this pub too long.

MRS. DORBELL, Eh?

LANCASTER (*throwing* MRS. DORBELL *out down* R.). Come on . . . and *this* time you're out for keeps!

MRS. DORBELL. Here, Harry Lancaster, you chucking me out? . . . Take your hands off me, Harry Lancaster! . . . etc.

(*She exits down* R. LANCASTER *remains by the door.*)

SARAH. Jack, is this true?

(JOE *clears up* R.)

JACK. Aye, it's true all right, Ma! And if you want to know, I am the child's father.

JANEY. What?

MRS. JENKINS. Well!

JACK (*turning to them*). So what?

JANEY (*across the table*). I won't let you go! Do you hear? And don't you forget it! I won't let you go!

JACK. Look here, Janey. . . .

JANEY. Don't you Janey me, Jack Hardacre.

SARAH (*moving up to* JACK'S L.). Never mind about her, Jack— you listen to me.

MRS. JENKINS (*crossing to* JACK'S R.). No, Jack Hardacre, you listen to me!

JACK. Well! Talk about blooming pincer movements. . . .

(MRS. JENKINS *crosses to the door down* R. *She takes* JANEY *with her, talking to her on the way.* SARAH *talks at the same time.*)

Go on! All of you! Have a go at me! And there was I in t' middle of the desert, saying, "Oh, to be home! Oh, to be home!"

JOE. I wish they'd kept you there.

MRS. JENKINS. The more fool her for not taking her chances that was offered her—and officers, too.

JANEY. But I've still got his ring. (*She turns.*) You'll marry me,

Jack Hardacre, if it's the last thing you do . . . and as for you, Milly Southern, you and your brat can. . . .

MILLY. One more crack about my child being a brat, and my coat comes off.

JANEY. He'll never marry you now.

JACK (*deliberately*). If I marry anybody else I'll be a bigamist.

JANEY. Do you mean to say you've been daft enough to marry her just because she's going to have a baby?

JACK. I married her the day my leave ended—and *I* bought the ring she's got.

JANEY. Oh!

MRS. JENKINS. The more fool her for not taking her chances.

JOE. She's not the only one. I've had chances, too. Well, I'm not staying here to be made a fool of. I'm off.

MRS. JENKINS (*to* JOE). Aye, that's right, lad! (*She takes* JOE'S *arm and persuades him out down* R.) You come along with us, Joe, to a respectable house. Our Janey'll make you a nice cup o' tea. Come on, Janey.

(JOE *and* MRS. JENKINS *go out down* R.)

LANCASTER (*moving to* R. C.). They're waiting for you, Janey.

JANEY. You shut your trap, you interfering swine! And as for you, Jack Hardacre, you're mad if you think I just stopped at home fretting for you while you were away. There's plenty more fish in the sea, and not stinking fish, either! (*She turns to the door down* R.)

MILLY. Janey—don't forget to take the ring.

JANEY (*turning*). You can have the lousy thing, and much good may it do you! (*She throws it at* MILLY.) And what's more, Jack Hardacre, I've not finished with you. I'll see your Colonel. There's martial law in the army, remember!

(*She exits down* R.)

JACK. Well, Ma, I've done it—should I have done? You see, Harry—fate accomply.

LANCASTER. Well, Sarah! Well, well, well!

SARAH (*to* LANCASTER). You keep out of this and then. . . .

(*Exit* LANCASTER C.)

. . . perhaps Ma can have a word.

JACK (*sitting on the bench,* L. *end*). If you ask me, Ma, it's too late for talk now.

(MILLY *sits* R. *of* JACK. LANCASTER *comes downstage behind the counter.*)

LANCASTER. That's true, Jack lad. Nowt to grumble at. (*He rubs his hands and beams.*) I'm quite satisfied.

SARAH. Oh, you are, are you? Not so fast, Harry Lancaster, or there'll be trouble.

LANCASTER. When a man's got a woman on his mind he'll stop at nowt. Look at your Jack and Milly.

SARAH. Why! Do you mean to say that's your idea wi' me?

LANCASTER. I said a feller'll stop at nowt.

SARAH. A woman neither. . . . (*She reaches for a glass to throw at him.*)

LANCASTER (*catching her arm*). Nay, nay, lass. These can't be replaced.

SARAH. Neither can my best plate.

LANCASTER. Oh, never mind about that. As for your best plate, I've told thee, I've got a pre-war Staffordshire service locked up in the china cupboard.

SARAH. Oh, don't start that all over again. I'm going home. Good night.

LANCASTER. No, Sally—don't thee go, lass.

JACK. Here, here, what is all this?

SARAH (*turning to* LANCASTER *by upstage stool*). What did you call me?

LANCASTER. Sally. What's wrong wi' that?

SARAH. Nowt. Takes me back a bit, that's all. My dad used to call me that.

LANCASTER. I wish I'd known you then.

SARAH. Well, you didn't.

MILLY. Stop fighting him, Mrs. Hardacre.

JACK (*puzzled*). But what the dickens. . . ?

LANCASTER. It's always the same, Jack. As soon as we get a bit sentimental. . . .

SARAH. It's nowt but a business transaction. Do you hear, Harry Lancaster?

JACK. Well, what is it, anyway?

LANCASTER. It's a country pub down in t' South. I've got an option on it, and I thought—me and thy mother, like. . . .

JACK (*eagerly*). A country pub? Down in t' South? (*He rises.*) Do you want a chucker-out?

SARAH. Oh, don't be daft. We want a bringer-in. This is business.

LANCASTER. Oh, Sally, lass. Don't you see? Jack and Milly could come with us. We'd give 'em a share. And think of it . . . your grandchild growing up in the country and having summat to look forward to. Aw, Sal! Come on, now. Come thee on!

JACK. Go on, Ma. There's not many grandmothers get chances like this, y'know. Go on, put the lad out of his misery.

SARAH (*after a little show of reluctance*). Aw. Well—all right, then. (*She sits back on to the upstage stool.*)

JACK. Hurray!

LANCASTER. At last! We'll have the biggest beano. . . . (*Excitedly.*) I've got a few bottles o' pre-war tucked away for the armistice. Let's take one round to your house to celebrate.

SARAH. Oh, all right, but you can keep the pre-war stuff for the armistice it belongs to. Half a pint of beer's good enough for this celebration. And a Guinness for madam over there.

JACK. Wheel 'em in, Harry! Wheel 'em in!

LANCASTER. It's after time, you know.

SARAH. What's that got to do with it?

LANCASTER. It can't be done.

(SARAH *exits* C. *through the Public Bar and comes downstage behind the counter.*)

SARAH. Who says it can't? Out of my way. (*She pushes* LANCASTER *downstage and puts a Guinness on the counter.*) Serve that out to Milly. (*She works the beer engine.*) I've always wanted to work one of these things.

(JACK *gives the Guinness to* MILLY.)

(*She pushes the bitter towards* JACK.) There you are, Jack, lad! On the house.

JACK (*sitting on the bench*). On the house! Blimey! Givin' it away!

LANCASTER. Fine start this is.

SARAH. Who's wearin' the trousers?

LANCASTER. Oh! If you want to put it *that* way. . . .

SARAH. Come on. (*She winks at* LANCASTER *and jerks her head towards the Public Bar.*) Let's be looking at that Staffordshire china you've been on about. Come on, shift your shins! (*She pulls* LANCASTER *upstage.*)

LANCASTER. Oh! I see what you mean.

(SARAH *and* LANCASTER *go off upstage.*)

JACK. Well, isn't that a bit of all right?

MILLY. It's just like your mother.

JACK. Terror, isn't she? Did you notice how she got that one in quick about wearing the trousers? I reckon he was daft to let her get away with that.

MILLY. What's daft about it? Nothing wrong with it as far as I can see.

JACK. Oh, there isn't, isn't there?

MILLY. Now don't start an argument. There's something more important than that. Look, there's the ring.

JACK. Where?

MILLY. There!

JACK. Thank God it's where it is, and not where it was.

MILLY. Well. Go on, pick it up.

JACK. Aw. Leave it for t' sweeper-up. *We* don't want the blooming thing. I'll have nowt second-hand on thee.

MILLY. Who said I wanted to wear it? My child's going to have an education. If that ring cost five pounds before the war it'll fetch ten now. Money's money. I've lived in Lancashire, tha knows. Go on, now. Pick it up.

JACK (*rising*). Pick it up? Must I? Must I really? (*He turns.*) I won't.

MILLY. I think you might pick it up when I ask you.

JACK (*by the counter; facing her*). Milly! Millicent Hardacre! Milly, lovey. Do you see what these are? They're trousers, and I'm wearing 'em. And I'm going to keep on wearing 'em from first to last. I'll work for you, I'll work my fingers to the bone, and you can have all my points and coupons and welcome, but so long as we're wed, you may as well know it now, I'm wearing the breeches and no one else. Now . . . there's the blooming ring. If you want it, you'll have to pick it up yourself. Come on, pick it up. Get on your pins, there's a good girl.

(MILLY *rises and moves round the table to* R. C.)

Pick it up. Come on, now. Pick it up, and stop messing about.

MILLY. Right, sergeant. (*She salutes and crosses towards the counter.*)

JACK (*stopping her as she is about to pick it up*). Milly, Milly. Sit down. (*Sitting her down.*) Fancy me forgetting. Here, drink up your Guinness, it'll do you good. Sup it up. Go on! (*He picks up the ring.*) Now don't ever let me clap eyes on that again, and remember, I only picked it up because. . . .

MILLY. I know, Jack.

SARAH (*from the Public Bar*). Give over, Lancaster. Half of that'll do.

JACK. Hey, you two—(*he knocks on the counter with a mug*)—no shinanigin! (*He turns to* MILLY.) Kiss me.

CURTAIN

FURNITURE AND PROPERTY PLOT

ACT I

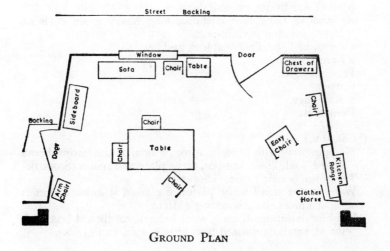

GROUND PLAN

On Stage:

Armchair. *In it:* Cushion.

Sideboard. *On it:* Runner, tray, 2 vases of flowers, cruet, work-basket with scissors, needle, cotton, thimble.

In it: Salt, pepper, mustard, glass sugar bowl, dessert spoon, patterned tablecloth, 3 soup plates, 3 large patterned plates, 1 large painted plate.

In each drawer: 1 Duster.

Sofa. *On it:* MILLY's coat, book.

Chest-of-drawers. *On it:* Runner, radio, book, menus, newspaper.

Easy chair.

Upright chair. *On it:* MILLY's skirt.

Under it: MILLY's shoes.

Table, up C. *On it:* Cloth, plant, photograph.

Chair, up C.

Kitchen table. *On it:* Ironing blanket, sheet, damping cloth, iron-stand, iron, glove, MILLY's blouse.
In drawer: White tablecloth, 3 dessert spoons, 3 forks, 3 knives.
3 Upright chairs round table.
Clothes-horse. *On it:* Freshly ironed underclothes.
Kitchen range. *On it:* Kettle, iron.
Mantelpiece. *On it:* 2 Silver cups, 2 vases, 2 photographs, clock.
Overmantel. *On it:* 4 Silver cups.
Fender, fire-irons.
Hooks above and below fire. *On downstage hook:* Oven cloth.
8 Pictures.
Map of war fronts, on wall down R.
At window: Long lace curtains, long heavy green curtains, blind, wooden curtain-pole.
On door, up L. C.*:* Practical lock and key.
2 Lamp brackets.
Pendant light.
Carpet.
2 Rag rugs.
Door mat.

Off Stage R.*:*
Shopping bag with parcels, apron, 2 small white basins, bread board, loaf, knife, hot-pot, large plate and spoon (SARAH).
Telegram, bookie's case, (CHARLIE).
Water-jug, 2 small white plates, 2 glasses, 3 forks, 2 dessert spoons, 2 knives, hat, hangbag (MILLY).
Webbing equipment, mug, steel helmet, cardboard box with shawl, small cardboard box, kitbag, rifle, cap (JACK).

Personal:
JACK: Cigarettes, lighter.

ACT II

SCENE 1

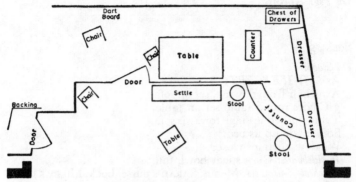

GROUND PLAN

On Stage:

Counter. *On it:* Glass of water, silver mug, beer-engine (two
   pulls), tray with jug of water, ash-tray, advertisement tray
   with 12 pony glasses, 1 glass mug and 1 larger glass, small
   cask on stand, drying cloth over cask.

Under it: 6 Glasses of bitter, 6 empty ½-pint bottles, 1 empty
   Guinness bottle, 1 full Guinness bottle, crate of bottles,
   counter cloth, glass cloth.

2 High stools.

Long bench or settle.

Small table. *On it:* Silver mug, ash-tray, mat.

Chair.

Stuffed fish in glass case, over door down R.

Dresser, downstage. *On it:* top shelf: Vase of imitation flowers,
   bottles, small glasses.

Middle shelf: Bottles, paper doilys, packets of cigarettes.

Bottom shelf: Empty glass, notebook and pencil, bottle of port,
   bottle of gin, ash-tray, 2 wine glasses, 3 pint mugs on hooks.

Dresser upstage. *On it: top shelf:* Bottles.

Middle shelf: 4 Reversed bottles with drip cups.

Bottom shelf: Cash register with notes and coins in it, tray with
   bottle of port and glass.

Chest-of-drawers. *On it:* Radio, pot of hydrangea. (*Left on from
   ACT I.*)

Small counter, upstage.

Table, upstage. (*Left on from ACT I.*)

2 Chairs. (*Left on from ACT I.*)

Dart board.

Framed advertisements and sporting prints as required.
Door mat, down R.
Large mat, C.

On Peg: Apron.

SCENE 2

On Stage:
    As ACT I, *EXCEPT*:
    Armchair from down R. set on sofa.
    3 Chairs round table set on table.
    Table pushed upstage towards sofa.
    Sofa made up as bed.
    Window curtains closed.
    In sideboard: Glass sugar bowl, full.
    On chest-of-drawers: Menus, SARAH's purse, book, MILLY's handbag, MILLY's hat.
    On clothes-horse: MILLY's underclothes.
    On chair above fire: Milly's skirt. *Under it:* MILLY's shoes.

Off Stage R.:
    White cup, purse (MRS. DORBELL).
    Kettle, tin hip bath and facecloth, coat (SARAH).
    Kitbag (JACK).
    Shoes, wrapped (MILLY).

ACT III

On Stage:
    As ACT II, SCENE I, *EXCEPT*:
    On table C.: Glass of bitter.
    On counter: Glass of water, silver mug, jug of water, beer engine, coins, pony glass with single Scotch, ash-tray, mat, ash-tray, tray with 11 pony glasses, glass mug and large Guinness glass, barrel, glass cloth.
    Under counter: As ACT II with ½-pint bottle of Guinness, ½-pint of beer.
    On downstage dresser, bottom shelf; add: Packet of cigarettes.

Personal:
    JOE: Cigarette.

LIGHTING PLOT

ACT I

F.O.H. Spots to cover downstage acting areas. (*Suitable colours are 7 Light Rose, 17 Steel Blue, 36 Pink.*)

Stage Spots to cover upstage acting areas—sideboard, round table R. C., door up L. C. and easy chair L. C. (*Suitable colours are 7 Light Rose, 17 Steel Blue, 36 Pink.*)

Floats: *18 Blue, 7 Light Rose.*

Fire Spot (*6 Red, broken in the centre to allow white light to throw*): Trained on face sitting back in easy chair.

Outside window and door; above door, *Amber* and *White* strip; above each side of window, *Amber* and *White* strips; outside L. of window Pageant Lamp (*51 Gold Tint*) to throw on face standing one step inside front door.

ACT II

Scene 1

F.O.H. Spots to cover downstage acting areas.

Stage Spots to cover corner up R., bench C., stool upstage at counter and behind counter. (*Colours as in ACT I.*)

Floats: *18 Blue, 7 Light Rose.*

Pendants in Public Bar: Two small bulbs behind cut-out lamps to show through panels in the top of the partition.

In Public Bar: Pageant Lamp (*51 Gold Tint*) to throw on back of painted canvas partition; Flood (*7 Light Rose*) on back wall.

Cue. At end of Scene: Black Out.

Scene 2

As for ACT I, *EXCEPT*: Stage Spots to cover chairs round table R. C., and easy chair only.

Chandelier and Wall Brackets ON.

NOTE: No outside lighting.

ACT III

As for ACT II, Scene 1.

Cue. Janey: "... Whose young man do you think he is?" Snap out lights in Public Bar. First Pendants, then Pageant and Flood.